Sonny Parsons

A GIFT FOR:

FROM:

DATE:

Published in Nashville, Tennessee, by Thomas Nelson. Thomas Nelson is a registered trademark of HarperCollins Christian Publishing, Inc.

Thomas Nelson titles may be purchased in bulk for educational, business, fund-raising, or sales promotional use. For information, please e-mail SpecialMarkets@ThomasNelson.com.

Scripture quotations are taken from the Holy Bible, New International Version®, NIV®. Copyright © 1973, 1978, 1984, 2011 by Biblica, Inc.™ Used by permission of Zondervan. All rights reserved worldwide. www.zondervan.com

ISBN-13: 978-1-4003-2309-8
ISBN-13: 978-0-310-62631-2 (custom)

Printed in the United States of America

16 17 18 19 20 RRD 6 5 4 3 2 1

God's
Promises®
for Men

NIV

COMPILED BY
JACK COUNTRYMAN

COUNTRYMAN®

A Division of Thomas Nelson Publishers

THOMAS NELSON

Since 1798

Contents

GOD REJOICES WHEN MEN . . .

DYNAMIC EXAMPLES OF GODLY MEN

Introduction

God desires to guide you to be a man after His own heart. He provides promises from Scripture that speak specifically to your needs, giving direction and answers so you can live a life filled with courage, hope, wisdom, and peace. God has given us an open invitation to come into His presence and find blessings through His promises. God understands the challenges you face and offers the gift of His Word to give spiritual insight and guidance. May *God's Promises® for Men NIV* encourage you in your daily walk.

God
Freely Gives
to Men . . .

Eternal Hope for Life

Sing to the LORD with grateful praise;
 make music to our God on the harp.

He covers the sky with clouds;
 he supplies the earth with rain
 and makes grass grow on the hills.
He provides food for the cattle
 and for the young ravens when they call.

His pleasure is not in the strength of the horse,
 nor his delight in the legs of the warrior;
the LORD delights in those who fear him,
 who put their hope in his unfailing love.

Extol the LORD, Jerusalem;
 praise your God, Zion.

He strengthens the bars of your gates
 and blesses your people within you.

PSALM 147:7–13

Since, then, you have been raised with Christ, set your hearts on things above, where Christ is, seated at the right hand of God. Set your minds on things above, not on earthly things. For you died, and your life is now hidden with Christ in God. When Christ, who is your life, appears, then you also will appear with him in glory.

Colossians 3:1–4

I have fought the good fight, I have finished the race, I have kept the faith. Now there is in store for me the crown of righteousness, which the Lord, the righteous Judge, will award to me on that day—and not only to me, but also to all who have longed for his appearing.

2 Timothy 4:7–8

Faith and love . . . spring from the hope stored up for you in heaven . . . about which you have already heard in the true message of the gospel that has come to you. In the same way, the gospel is bearing fruit and growing throughout the whole world—just as it has been doing among you since the day you heard it and truly understood God's grace.

Colossians 1:5–6

But since we belong to the day, let us be sober, putting on faith and love as a breastplate, and the hope of salvation as a helmet. For God did not appoint us to suffer wrath but to receive salvation through our Lord Jesus Christ. He died for us so that, whether we are awake or asleep, we may live together with him. Therefore encourage one another and build each other up, just as in fact you are doing.

1 Thessalonians 5:8–11

For those who are led by the Spirit of God are the children of God. The Spirit you received does not make you slaves, so that you live in fear again; rather, the Spirit you received brought about your adoption to sonship. And by him we cry, "Abba, Father." The Spirit himself testifies with our spirit that we are God's children. Now if we are children, then we are heirs—heirs of God and co-heirs with Christ, if indeed we share in his sufferings in order that we may also share in his glory.

I consider that our present sufferings are not worth comparing with the glory that will be revealed in us.

Romans 8:14–18

But because of his great love for us, God, who is rich in mercy, made us alive with Christ even when we were dead in transgressions—it is by grace you have been saved. And God raised us up with Christ and seated us with him in the heavenly realms in Christ Jesus, in order that in the coming ages he might show the incomparable riches of his grace, expressed in his kindness to us in Christ Jesus. For it is by grace you have been saved, through faith—and this is not from yourselves, it is the gift of God.

EPHESIANS 2:4–8

Know that a person is not justified by the works of the law, but by faith in Jesus Christ. So we, too, have put our faith in Christ Jesus that we may be justified by faith in Christ and not by the works of the law, because by the works of the law no one will be justified. . . .

For through the law I died to the law so that I might live for God. I have been crucified with Christ and I no longer live, but Christ lives in me. The life I now live in the body, I live by faith in the Son of God, who loved me and gave himself for me.

GALATIANS 2:16, 19–20

Praise be to the God and Father of our Lord Jesus Christ! In his great mercy he has given us new birth into a living hope through the resurrection of Jesus Christ from the dead, and into an inheritance that can never perish, spoil or fade. This inheritance is kept in heaven for you, who through faith are shielded by God's power until the coming of the salvation that is ready to be revealed in the last time. In all this you greatly rejoice, though now for a little while you may have had to suffer grief in all kinds of trials. These have come so that the proven genuineness of your faith—of greater worth than gold, which perishes even though refined by fire—may result in praise, glory and honor when Jesus Christ is revealed. Though you have not seen him, you love him; and even though you do not see him now, you believe in him and are filled with an inexpressible and glorious joy, for you are receiving the end result of your faith, the salvation of your souls.

1 Peter 1:3–9

Wisdom for Each Day

My son, pay attention to my wisdom,
   turn your ear to my words of insight,
that you may maintain discretion
   and your lips may preserve knowledge.

PROVERBS 5:1–2

The fear of the LORD is the beginning of wisdom;
   all who follow his precepts have good
      understanding.
   To him belongs eternal praise.

PSALM 111:10

How much better to get wisdom than gold,
   to get insight rather than silver!

PROVERBS 16:16

Our days may come to seventy years,
    or eighty, if our strength endures;
yet the best of them are but trouble and sorrow,
    for they quickly pass, and we fly away.
If only we knew the power of your anger!
    Your wrath is as great as the fear that is your due.
Teach us to number our days,
    that we may gain a heart of wisdom.

PSALM 90:10–12

But the wisdom that comes from heaven is first of all pure; then peace-loving, considerate, submissive, full of mercy and good fruit, impartial and sincere. Peacemakers who sow in peace reap a harvest of righteousness.

JAMES 3:17–18

The fear of the LORD is the beginning of wisdom,
    and knowledge of the Holy One is understanding.
For through wisdom your days will be many,
    and years will be added to your life.
If you are wise, your wisdom will reward you;
    if you are a mocker, you alone will suffer.

PROVERBS 9:10–12

Get wisdom, get understanding;
 do not forget my words or turn away from them.
Do not forsake wisdom, and she will protect you;
 love her, and she will watch over you.
The beginning of wisdom is this: Get wisdom.
 Though it cost all you have, get understanding.
Cherish her, and she will exalt you;
 embrace her, and she will honor you.
She will give you a garland to grace your head
 and present you with a glorious crown.

Listen, my son, accept what I say,
 and the years of your life will be many.
I instruct you in the way of wisdom
 and lead you along straight paths.

PROVERBS 4:5–11

If any of you lacks wisdom, you should ask God, who gives generously to all without finding fault, and it will be given to you. But when you ask, you must believe and not doubt, because the one who doubts is like a wave of the sea, blown and tossed by the wind.

JAMES 1:5–6

Blessed are those who find wisdom,
    those who gain understanding,
for she is more profitable than silver
    and yields better returns than gold.
She is more precious than rubies;
    nothing you desire can compare with her.
Long life is in her right hand;
    in her left hand are riches and honor.
Her ways are pleasant ways,
    and all her paths are peace.
She is a tree of life to those who take hold of her;
    those who hold her fast will be blessed.

By wisdom the LORD laid the earth's foundations,
    by understanding he set the heavens in place;
by his knowledge the watery depths were divided,
    and the clouds let drop the dew.

My son, do not let wisdom and understanding out of
        your sight,
    preserve sound judgment and discretion;
they will be life for you,
    an ornament to grace your neck.
Then you will go on your way in safety,
    and your foot will not stumble.

PROVERBS 3:13–23

We do, however, speak a message of wisdom among the mature, but not the wisdom of this age or of the rulers of this age, who are coming to nothing. No, we declare God's wisdom, a mystery that has been hidden and that God destined for our glory before time began. None of the rulers of this age understood it, for if they had, they would not have crucified the Lord of glory. However, as it is written:

"What no eye has seen,
    what no ear has heard,
and what no human mind has conceived"—
    the things God has prepared for those who
        love him.

1 CORINTHIANS 2:6–9

Victory over Sin

—◆—

Therefore, if anyone is in Christ, the new creation has come: The old has gone, the new is here! All this is from God, who reconciled us to himself through Christ and gave us the ministry of reconciliation: that God was reconciling the world to himself in Christ, not counting people's sins against them. And he has committed to us the message of reconciliation. We are therefore Christ's ambassadors, as though God were making his appeal through us. We implore you on Christ's behalf: Be reconciled to God. God made him who had no sin to be sin for us, so that in him we might become the righteousness of God.

2 CORINTHIANS 5:17–21

You, God, know my folly;
    my guilt is not hidden from you.

PSALM 69:5

Wash and make yourselves clean.
　　Take your evil deeds out of my sight;
　　stop doing wrong.
Learn to do right; seek justice.
　　Defend the oppressed.
Take up the cause of the fatherless;
　　plead the case of the widow.

"Come now, let us settle the matter,"
　　says the LORD.
"Though your sins are like scarlet,
　　they shall be as white as snow;
though they are red as crimson,
　　they shall be like wool.
If you are willing and obedient,
　　you will eat the good things of the land."

ISAIAH 1:16–19

For all who rely on the works of the law are under a curse, as it is written: "Cursed is everyone who does not continue to do everything written in the Book of the Law." Clearly no one who relies on the law is justified before God, because "the righteous will live by faith."

GALATIANS 3:10–11

But you know that he appeared so that he might take away our sins. And in him is no sin. No one who lives in him keeps on sinning. No one who continues to sin has either seen him or known him.

Dear children, do not let anyone lead you astray. The one who does what is right is righteous, just as he is righteous.

1 JOHN 3:5–7

"Where, O death, is your victory?
Where, O death, is your sting?"

The sting of death is sin, and the power of sin is the law. But thanks be to God! He gives us the victory through our Lord Jesus Christ.

Therefore, my dear brothers . . . stand firm. Let nothing move you. Always give yourselves fully to the work of the Lord, because you know that your labor in the Lord is not in vain.

1 CORINTHIANS 15:55–58

Finally, be strong in the Lord and in his mighty power. Put on the full armor of God, so that you can take your stand against the devil's schemes. For our struggle is not against flesh and blood, but against the rulers, against the authorities, against the powers of this dark world and against the spiritual forces of evil in the heavenly realms. Therefore put on the full armor of God, so that when the day of evil comes, you may be able to stand your ground, and after you have done everything, to stand. Stand firm then, with the belt of truth buckled around your waist, with the breastplate of righteousness in place, and with your feet fitted with the readiness that comes from the gospel of peace. In addition to all this, take up the shield of faith, with which you can extinguish all the flaming arrows of the evil one. Take the helmet of salvation and the sword of the Spirit, which is the word of God.

And pray in the Spirit on all occasions with all kinds of prayers and requests. With this in mind, be alert and always keep on praying for all the Lord's people.

EPHESIANS 6:10–18

Peace in Troubled Times

Whoever regards one day as special does so to the Lord. Whoever eats meat does so to the Lord, for they give thanks to God; and whoever abstains does so to the Lord and gives thanks to God. For none of us lives for ourselves alone, and none of us dies for ourselves alone. If we live, we live for the Lord; and if we die, we die for the Lord. So, whether we live or die, we belong to the Lord.

ROMANS 14:6–8

Turn to me and be gracious to me,
 for I am lonely and afflicted.
Relieve the troubles of my heart
 and free me from my anguish.
Look on my affliction and my distress
 and take away all my sins.

PSALM 25:16–18

A horse is a vain hope for deliverance;
 despite all its great strength it cannot save.
But the eyes of the LORD are on those who fear him,
 on those whose hope is in his unfailing love,
to deliver them from death
 and keep them alive in famine.

We wait in hope for the LORD;
 he is our help and our shield.
In him our hearts rejoice,
 for we trust in his holy name.
May your unfailing love be with us, LORD,
 even as we put our hope in you.

         PSALM 33:17–22

The LORD builds up Jerusalem;
 he gathers the exiles of Israel.
He heals the brokenhearted
 and binds up their wounds. . . .

Great is our Lord and mighty in power;
 his understanding has no limit.
The LORD sustains the humble
 but casts the wicked to the ground.

        PSALM 147:2–3, 5–6

"Peace I leave with you; my peace I give you. I do not give to you as the world gives. Do not let your hearts be troubled and do not be afraid."

JOHN 14:27

Cast all your anxiety on him because he cares for you.

Be alert and of sober mind. Your enemy the devil prowls around like a roaring lion looking for some-one to devour. Resist him, standing firm in the faith, because you know that the family of believers throughout the world is undergoing the same kind of sufferings.

And the God of all grace, who called you to his eternal glory in Christ, after you have suffered a little while, will himself restore you and make you strong, firm and steadfast. To him be the power for ever and ever. Amen.

1 PETER 5:7–11

Trust in the LORD with all your heart
and lean not on your own understanding;
in all your ways submit to him,
and he will make your paths straight.

PROVERBS 3:5–6

I will be glad and rejoice in your love,
  for you saw my affliction
  and knew the anguish of my soul.

PSALM 31:7

I will extol the LORD at all times;
  his praise will always be on my lips.
I will glory in the LORD;
  let the afflicted hear and rejoice.
Glorify the LORD with me;
  let us exalt his name together.

I sought the LORD, and he answered me;
  he delivered me from all my fears.
Those who look to him are radiant;
  their faces are never covered with shame.
This poor man called, and the LORD heard him;
  he saved him out of all his troubles.
The angel of the LORD encamps around those who
      fear him,
  and he delivers them.

Taste and see that the LORD is good;
  blessed is the one who takes refuge in him.

PSALM 34:1–8

Power to Defeat Their Deepest Fears

———◆◆◆———

When Jesus spoke again to the people, he said, "I am the light of the world. Whoever follows me will never walk in darkness, but will have the light of life."

JOHN 8:12

I love you, LORD, my strength.

The LORD is my rock, my fortress and my deliverer;
    my God is my rock, in whom I take refuge,
    my shield and the horn of my salvation, my
        stronghold.

I called to the LORD, who is worthy of praise,
    and I have been saved from my enemies.

PSALM 18:1–3

You, LORD, keep my lamp burning;
    my God turns my darkness into light.
With your help I can advance against a troop;
    with my God I can scale a wall.

As for God, his way is perfect:
    The LORD's word is flawless;
    he shields all who take refuge in him.
For who is God besides the LORD?
    And who is the Rock except our God?

PSALM 18:28–31

Have no fear of sudden disaster
    or of the ruin that overtakes the wicked,
for the LORD will be at your side
    and will keep your foot from being snared.

PROVERBS 3:25–26

The fear of the LORD is the beginning of wisdom;
    all who follow his precepts have good
        understanding.
    To him belongs eternal praise.

PSALM 111:10

The LORD is my light and my salvation—
　　whom shall I fear?
The LORD is the stronghold of my life—
　　of whom shall I be afraid?

When the wicked advance against me
　　to devour me,
it is my enemies and my foes
　　who will stumble and fall.
Though an army besiege me,
　　my heart will not fear;
though war break out against me,
　　even then I will be confident.

One thing I ask from the LORD,
　　this only do I seek:
that I may dwell in the house of the LORD
　　all the days of my life,
to gaze on the beauty of the LORD
　　and to seek him in his temple.
For in the day of trouble
　　he will keep me safe in his dwelling;
he will hide me in the shelter of his sacred tent
　　and set me high upon a rock.

PSALM 27:1–5

What, then, shall we say in response to these things? If God is for us, who can be against us? He who did not spare his own Son, but gave him up for us all—how will he not also, along with him, graciously give us all things? Who will bring any charge against those whom God has chosen? It is God who justifies. Who then is the one who condemns? No one. Christ Jesus who died—more than that, who was raised to life—is at the right hand of God and is also interceding for us. Who shall separate us from the love of Christ? Shall trouble or hardship or persecution or famine or nakedness or danger or sword? As it is written:

"For your sake we face death all day long;
    we are considered as sheep to be slaughtered."

No, in all these things we are more than conquerors through him who loved us. For I am convinced that neither death nor life, neither angels nor demons, neither the present nor the future, nor any powers, neither height nor depth, nor anything else in all creation, will be able to separate us from the love of God that is in Christ Jesus our Lord.

ROMANS 8:31–39

Courage to Be Men of Integrity

❖

The LORD detests dishonest scales,
　but accurate weights find favor with him.

When pride comes, then comes disgrace,
　but with humility comes wisdom.

The integrity of the upright guides them,
　but the unfaithful are destroyed by their
　　duplicity.

PROVERBS 11:1–3

If I have walked with falsehood
　or my foot has hurried after deceit—
let God weigh me in honest scales
　and he will know that I am blameless.

JOB 31:5–6

Blessed is the one
>who does not walk in step with the wicked
or stand in the way that sinners take
>or sit in the company of mockers,
but whose delight is in the law of the LORD,
>and who meditates on his law day and night.
That person is like a tree planted by streams of water,
>which yields its fruit in season
and whose leaf does not wither—
>whatever they do prospers.

Not so the wicked!
>They are like chaff
>that the wind blows away.
Therefore the wicked will not stand in the judgment,
>nor sinners in the assembly of the righteous.

For the LORD watches over the way of the righteous,
>but the way of the wicked leads to destruction.

PSALM 1:1–6

The righteous lead blameless lives;
>blessed are their children after them.

PROVERBS 20:7

An honest witness tells the truth,
> but a false witness tells lies.

The words of the reckless pierce like swords,
> but the tongue of the wise brings healing.

Truthful lips endure forever,
> but a lying tongue lasts only a moment.

PROVERBS 12:17–19

And Job continued his discourse:

"As surely as God lives, who has denied me justice,
> the Almighty, who has made my life bitter,
as long as I have life within me,
> the breath of God in my nostrils,
my lips will not say anything wicked,
> and my tongue will not utter lies.
I will never admit you are in the right;
> till I die, I will not deny my integrity.
I will maintain my innocence and never let go of it;
> my conscience will not reproach me as long as
> > I live."

JOB 27:1–6

Good will come to those who are generous and
      lend freely,
  who conduct their affairs with justice.

Surely the righteous will never be shaken;
  they will be remembered forever.
They will have no fear of bad news;
  their hearts are steadfast, trusting in the LORD.

PSALM 112:5–7

Let the LORD judge the peoples.
Vindicate me, LORD, according to my righteousness,
  according to my integrity, O Most High.
Bring to an end the violence of the wicked
  and make the righteous secure—
you, the righteous God
  who probes minds and hearts.

PSALM 7:8–9

God Asks

Men *to* . . .

Witness to the Lost

—◦◆◦—

"Therefore go and make disciples of all nations, baptizing them in the name of the Father and of the Son and of the Holy Spirit, and teaching them to obey everything I have commanded you. And surely I am with you always, to the very end of the age."

MATTHEW 28:19–20

"The Spirit of the Lord is on me,
    because he has anointed me
    to proclaim good news to the poor.
He has sent me to proclaim freedom for the
      prisoners
    and recovery of sight for the blind,
to set the oppressed free,
    to proclaim the year of the Lord's favor."

LUKE 4:18–19

Therefore God exalted him to the highest place
    and gave him the name that is above every name,
that at the name of Jesus every knee should bow,
    in heaven and on earth and under the earth,
and every tongue acknowledge that Jesus Christ
        is Lord,
    to the glory of God the Father.

PHILIPPIANS 2:9–11

"Whoever publicly acknowledges me before others, the Son of Man will also acknowledge before the angels of God. But whoever disowns me before others will be disowned before the angels of God."

LUKE 12:8–9

"I tell you that in the same way there will be more rejoicing in heaven over one sinner who repents than over ninety-nine righteous persons who do not need to repent."

LUKE 15:7

"For the Son of Man came to seek and to save the lost."

LUKE 19:10

"Whoever acknowledges me before others, I will also acknowledge before my Father in heaven. But whoever disowns me before others, I will disown before my Father in heaven."

MATTHEW 10:32–33

"Here I am! I stand at the door and knock. If anyone hears my voice and opens the door, I will come in and eat with that person, and they with me."

REVELATION 3:20

"Whoever serves me must follow me; and where I am, my servant also will be. My Father will honor the one who serves me."

JOHN 12:26

"For God so loved the world that he gave his one and only Son, that whoever believes in him shall not perish but have eternal life. For God did not send his Son into the world to condemn the world, but to save the world through him."

JOHN 3:16–17

The Lord is not slow in keeping his promise, as some understand slowness. Instead he is patient with you, not wanting anyone to perish, but everyone to come to repentance.

2 PETER 3:9

Those who are wise will shine like the brightness of the heavens, and those who lead many to righteousness, like the stars for ever and ever.

DANIEL 12:3

Love Their Neighbors

"You shall not give false testimony against your neighbor.

"You shall not covet your neighbor's house. You shall not covet your neighbor's wife, or his male or female servant, his ox or donkey, or anything that belongs to your neighbor."

EXODUS 20:16–17

It is a sin to despise one's neighbor,
 but blessed is the one who is kind to the needy.

PROVERBS 14:21

Do not bring hastily to court,
for what will you do in the end
 if your neighbor puts you to shame?

If you take your neighbor to court,
 do not betray another's confidence.

PROVERBS 25:8–9

But he wanted to justify himself, so he asked Jesus, "And who is my neighbor?"

In reply Jesus said: "A man was going down from Jerusalem to Jericho, when he was attacked by robbers. They stripped him of his clothes, beat him and went away, leaving him half dead. A priest happened to be going down the same road, and when he saw the man, he passed by on the other side. So too, a Levite, when he came to the place and saw him, passed by on the other side. But a Samaritan, as he traveled, came where the man was; and when he saw him, he took pity on him. He went to him and bandaged his wounds, pouring on oil and wine. Then he put the man on his own donkey, brought him to an inn and took care of him. The next day he took out two denarii and gave them to the innkeeper. 'Look after him,' he said, 'and when I return, I will reimburse you for any extra expense you may have.'

"Which of these three do you think was a neighbor to the man who fell into the hands of robbers?"

The expert in the law replied, "The one who had mercy on him."

Jesus told him, "Go and do likewise."

LUKE 10:29–37

"'Honor your father and mother,' and 'love your neighbor as yourself.'"

Whoever derides their neighbor has no sense,
    but the one who has understanding holds their
        tongue.

Whoever slanders their neighbor in secret,
    I will put to silence;
whoever has haughty eyes and a proud heart,
    I will not tolerate.

My eyes will be on the faithful in the land,
    that they may dwell with me;
the one whose walk is blameless
    will minister to me.

No one who practices deceit
    will dwell in my house;
no one who speaks falsely
    will stand in my presence.

Do not conform to the pattern of this world, but be transformed by the renewing of your mind. Then you will be able to test and approve what God's will is—his good, pleasing and perfect will.

For by the grace given me I say to every one of you: Do not think of yourself more highly than you ought, but rather think of yourself with sober judgment, in accordance with the faith God has distributed to each of you.

ROMANS 12:2–3

Do not say to your neighbor,
    "Come back tomorrow and I'll give it to you"—
    when you already have it with you.
Do not plot harm against your neighbor,
    who lives trustfully near you.

PROVERBS 3:28–29

Reach Out to the Poor and Homeless

—◆—

Whoever shuts their ears to the cry of the poor
will also cry out and not be answered.

PROVERBS 21:13

Keep on loving one another as brothers and sisters. Do not forget to show hospitality to strangers, for by so doing some people have shown hospitality to angels without knowing it.

HEBREWS 13:1–2

Above all, love each other deeply, because love covers over a multitude of sins. Offer hospitality to one another without grumbling. Each of you should use whatever gift you have received to serve others, as faithful stewards of God's grace in its various forms.

1 PETER 4:8–10

"Then the King will say to those on his right, 'Come, you who are blessed by my Father; take your inheritance, the kingdom prepared for you since the creation of the world. For I was hungry and you gave me something to eat, I was thirsty and you gave me something to drink, I was a stranger and you invited me in, I needed clothes and you clothed me, I was sick and you looked after me, I was in prison and you came to visit me.'

"Then the righteous will answer him, 'Lord, when did we see you hungry and feed you, or thirsty and give you something to drink? When did we see you a stranger and invite you in, or needing clothes and clothe you? When did we see you sick or in prison and go to visit you?'

"The King will reply, 'Truly I tell you, whatever you did for one of the least of these brothers and sisters of mine, you did for me.'"

MATTHEW 25:34–40

"Is it not to share your food with the hungry
    and to provide the poor wanderer with shelter—
when you see the naked, to clothe them,
    and not to turn away from your own flesh and
        blood?
Then your light will break forth like the dawn,
    and your healing will quickly appear;
then your righteousness will go before you,
    and the glory of the Lord will be your rear
        guard.
Then you will call, and the Lord will answer;
    you will cry for help, and he will say: Here am I.

"If you do away with the yoke of oppression,
    with the pointing finger and malicious talk,
and if you spend yourselves in behalf of the hungry
    and satisfy the needs of the oppressed,
then your light will rise in the darkness,
    and your night will become like the noonday.
The Lord will guide you always;
    he will satisfy your needs in a sun-scorched land
    and will strengthen your frame.
You will be like a well-watered garden,
    like a spring whose waters never fail."

Isaiah 58:7–11

But God will never forget the needy;
    the hope of the afflicted will never perish.

Arise, LORD, do not let mortals triumph;
    let the nations be judged in your presence.

PSALM 9:18–19

"When you reap the harvest of your land, do not reap to the very edges of your field or gather the gleanings of your harvest. Do not go over your vineyard a second time or pick up the grapes that have fallen. Leave them for the poor and the foreigner. I am the LORD your God."

LEVITICUS 19:9–10

If anyone has material possessions and sees a brother or sister in need but has no pity on them, how can the love of God be in that person? Dear children, let us not love with words or speech but with actions and in truth.

This is how we know that we belong to the truth and how we set our hearts at rest in his presence: If our hearts condemn us, we know that God is greater than our hearts, and he knows everything.

1 JOHN 3:17–20

Blessed are those whose help is the God of Jacob,
    whose hope is in the LORD their God.

He is the Maker of heaven and earth,
    the sea, and everything in them—
    he remains faithful forever.
He upholds the cause of the oppressed
    and gives food to the hungry.
The LORD sets prisoners free,
    the LORD gives sight to the blind,
the LORD lifts up those who are bowed down,
    the LORD loves the righteous.
The LORD watches over the foreigner
    and sustains the fatherless and the widow,
    but he frustrates the ways of the wicked.

The LORD reigns forever,
    your God, O Zion, for all generations.

Praise the LORD.

PSALM 146:5–10

Defend the weak and the fatherless;
   uphold the cause of the poor and the oppressed.
Rescue the weak and the needy;
   deliver them from the hand of the wicked.

PSALM 82:3–4

Suppose a brother or a sister is without clothes and daily food. If one of you says to them, "Go in peace; keep warm and well fed," but does nothing about their physical needs, what good is it? In the same way, faith by itself, if it is not accompanied by action, is dead.

JAMES 2:15–17

Trust God

———◆———

I lift up my eyes to the mountains—
    where does my help come from?
My help comes from the LORD,
    the Maker of heaven and earth.

He will not let your foot slip—
    he who watches over you will not slumber;
indeed, he who watches over Israel
    will neither slumber nor sleep.

The LORD watches over you—
    the LORD is your shade at your right hand;
the sun will not harm you by day,
    nor the moon by night.

The LORD will keep you from all harm—
    he will watch over your life;
the LORD will watch over your coming and going
    both now and forevermore.

PSALM 121:1–8

Oh, the depth of the riches of the wisdom and
     knowledge of God!
     How unsearchable his judgments,
     and his paths beyond tracing out!
"Who has known the mind of the Lord?
     Or who has been his counselor?"
"Who has ever given to God,
     that God should repay them?"
For from him and through him and for him are all
     things.
     To him be the glory forever! Amen.

ROMANS 11:33–36

When I am in distress, I call to you,
     because you answer me.

Among the gods there is none like you, Lord;
     no deeds can compare with yours.
All the nations you have made
     will come and worship before you, Lord;
     they will bring glory to your name.
For you are great and do marvelous deeds;
     you alone are God.

PSALM 86:7–10

Trust in the LORD with all your heart
  and lean not on your own understanding;
in all your ways submit to him,
  and he will make your paths straight.

PROVERBS 3:5–6

He said:

"The LORD is my rock, my fortress and my deliverer;
  my God is my rock, in whom I take refuge,
  my shield and the horn of my salvation.
He is my stronghold, my refuge and my savior—
  from violent people you save me."

2 SAMUEL 22:2–3

Though he slay me, yet will I hope in him;
  I will surely defend my ways to his face.
Indeed, this will turn out for my deliverance,
  for no godless person would dare come before
    him!

JOB 13:15–16

Know that the LORD has set apart his faithful
        servant for himself;
    the LORD hears when I call to him.

Tremble and do not sin;
    when you are on your beds,
    search your hearts and be silent.
Offer the sacrifices of the righteous
    and trust in the LORD.

PSALM 4:3–5

Keep me safe, my God,
    for in you I take refuge.

I say to the LORD, "You are my Lord;
    apart from you I have no good thing."

PSALM 16:1–2

Honor and Support Their Church and Pastors

———◆◇◆———

Now we ask you, brothers . . . to acknowledge those who work hard among you, who care for you in the Lord and who admonish you. Hold them in the highest regard in love because of their work. Live in peace with each other.

1 Thessalonians 5:12–13

Remember your leaders, who spoke the word of God to you. Consider the outcome of their way of life and imitate their faith. . . .

Have confidence in your leaders and submit to their authority, because they keep watch over you as those who must give an account. Do this so that their work will be a joy, not a burden, for that would be of no benefit to you.

Hebrews 13:7, 17

If we endure,
we will also reign with him.
If we disown him,
he will also disown us.

2 Timothy 2:12

Lord, who may dwell in your sacred tent?
Who may live on your holy mountain?

The one whose walk is blameless,
who does what is righteous,
who speaks the truth from their heart.

Psalm 15:1–2

In Christ you have been brought to fullness. He is the head over every power and authority. . . .

They have lost connection with the head, from whom the whole body, supported and held together by its ligaments and sinews, grows as God causes it to grow.

Colossians 2:10, 19

Just as a body, though one, has many parts, but all its many parts form one body, so it is with Christ. For we were all baptized by one Spirit so as to form one body—whether Jews or Gentiles, slave or free—and we were all given the one Spirit to drink. Even so the body is not made up of one part but of many.

Now if the foot should say, "Because I am not a hand, I do not belong to the body," it would not for that reason stop being part of the body. And if the ear should say, "Because I am not an eye, I do not belong to the body," it would not for that reason stop being part of the body. If the whole body were an eye, where would the sense of hearing be? If the whole body were an ear, where would the sense of smell be? But in fact God has placed the parts in the body, every one of them, just as he wanted them to be. If they were all one part, where would the body be? As it is, there are many parts, but one body.

The eye cannot say to the hand, "I don't need you!" And the head cannot say to the feet, "I don't need you!" On the contrary, those parts of the body that seem to be weaker are indispensable, and the parts that we think are less honorable we treat with special honor. And the parts that are unpresentable are treated with special modesty, while our presentable parts need no special treatment. But God has put the body together, giving greater honor to the parts that lacked it, so that there should be no division in the body, but that its parts should have equal concern for each other. If one part suffers, every part suffers with it; if one part is honored, every part rejoices with it.

Now you are the body of Christ, and each one of you is a part of it. And God has placed in the church first of all apostles, second prophets, third teachers, then miracles, then gifts of healing, of helping, of guidance, and of different kinds of tongues.

1 CORINTHIANS 12:12–28

In the same way, you who are younger, submit yourselves to your elders. All of you, clothe yourselves with humility toward one another, because,

"God opposes the proud
     but shows favor to the humble."

1 PETER 5:5

For just as each of us has one body with many members, and these members do not all have the same function, so in Christ we, though many, form one body, and each member belongs to all the others.

ROMANS 12:4–5

So Christ himself gave the apostles, the prophets, the evangelists, the pastors and teachers, to equip his people for works of service, so that the body of Christ may be built up.

EPHESIANS 4:11–12

God Gives
Men Strength
When . . .

They Comfort Their Loved Ones

—◆—

But from everlasting to everlasting
    the LORD's love is with those who fear him,
    and his righteousness with their children's
        children—
with those who keep his covenant
    and remember to obey his precepts.

PSALM 103:17–18

He tends his flock like a shepherd:
    He gathers the lambs in his arms
and carries them close to his heart;
    he gently leads those that have young.

ISAIAH 40:11

"Are not two sparrows sold for a penny? Yet not one of them will fall to the ground outside your Father's care. And even the very hairs of your head are all numbered. So don't be afraid; you are worth more than many sparrows."

MATTHEW 10:29–31

So do not fear, for I am with you;
  do not be dismayed, for I am your God.
I will strengthen you and help you;
  I will uphold you with my righteous right
    hand. . . .

"See, I will make you into a threshing sledge,
  new and sharp, with many teeth.
You will thresh the mountains and crush them,
  and reduce the hills to chaff.
You will winnow them, the wind will pick them up,
  and a gale will blow them away.
But you will rejoice in the LORD
  and glory in the Holy One of Israel.

ISAIAH 41:10, 15–16

The waves of death swirled about me;
  the torrents of destruction overwhelmed me.
The cords of the grave coiled around me;
  the snares of death confronted me.

In my distress I called to the LORD;
  I called out to my God.
From his temple he heard my voice;
  my cry came to his ears.

2 SAMUEL 22:5–7

Now we ask you, brothers . . . to acknowledge those who work hard among you, who care for you in the Lord and who admonish you. Hold them in the highest regard in love because of their work. Live in peace with each other. And we urge you, brothers . . . warn those who are idle and disruptive, encourage the disheartened, help the weak, be patient with everyone. Make sure that nobody pays back wrong for wrong, but always strive to do what is good for each other and for everyone else.

1 THESSALONIANS 5:12–15

May the God who gives endurance and encouragement give you the same attitude of mind toward each other that Christ Jesus had, so that with one mind and one voice you may glorify the God and Father of our Lord Jesus Christ.

Accept one another, then, just as Christ accepted you, in order to bring praise to God.

ROMANS 15:5–7

Shout for joy, you heavens;
    rejoice, you earth;
    burst into song, you mountains!
For the LORD comforts his people
    and will have compassion on his afflicted ones.

But Zion said, "The LORD has forsaken me,
    the Lord has forgotten me."

"Can a mother forget the baby at her breast
    and have no compassion on the child she has borne?
Though she may forget,
    I will not forget you!
See, I have engraved you on the palms of my hands;
    your walls are ever before me."

ISAIAH 49:13–16

Praise be to the God and Father of our Lord Jesus Christ, the Father of compassion and the God of all comfort, who comforts us in all our troubles, so that we can comfort those in any trouble with the comfort we ourselves receive from God. For just as we share abundantly in the sufferings of Christ, so also our comfort abounds through Christ.

2 CORINTHIANS 1:3–5

They Feel Defeated and Powerless

—◆—

God is our refuge and strength,
an ever-present help in trouble.
Therefore we will not fear, though the earth give way
and the mountains fall into the heart of the sea,
though its waters roar and foam
and the mountains quake with their surging.

There is a river whose streams make glad the city of
God,
the holy place where the Most High dwells.
God is within her, she will not fall;
God will help her at break of day.

PSALM 46:1–5

Hear me, Lord, and answer me,
  for I am poor and needy.
Guard my life, for I am faithful to you;
  save your servant who trusts in you.
You are my God; have mercy on me, Lord,
  for I call to you all day long.
Bring joy to your servant, Lord,
  for I put my trust in you.

You, Lord, are forgiving and good,
  abounding in love to all who call to you.
Hear my prayer, Lord;
  listen to my cry for mercy.
When I am in distress, I call to you,
  because you answer me.

PSALM 86:1–7

Trouble and distress have come upon me,
  but your commands give me delight.
Your statutes are always righteous;
  give me understanding that I may live.

PSALM 119:143–144

Whoever dwells in the shelter of the Most High
    will rest in the shadow of the Almighty.
I will say of the LORD, "He is my refuge and my fortress,
    my God, in whom I trust."

Surely he will save you
    from the fowler's snare
    and from the deadly pestilence.
He will cover you with his feathers,
    and under his wings you will find refuge;
    his faithfulness will be your shield and rampart.
You will not fear the terror of night,
    nor the arrow that flies by day,
nor the pestilence that stalks in the darkness,
    nor the plague that destroys at midday.
A thousand may fall at your side,
    ten thousand at your right hand,
    but it will not come near you.
You will only observe with your eyes
    and see the punishment of the wicked.

If you say, "The LORD is my refuge,"
    and you make the Most High your dwelling,
no harm will overtake you,
    no disaster will come near your tent.

PSALM 91:1–10

Three times I pleaded with the Lord to take it away from me. But he said to me, "My grace is sufficient for you, for my power is made perfect in weakness." Therefore I will boast all the more gladly about my weaknesses, so that Christ's power may rest on me. That is why, for Christ's sake, I delight in weaknesses, in insults, in hardships, in persecutions, in difficulties. For when I am weak, then I am strong.

2 CORINTHIANS 12:8–10

And so it was with me, brothers. . . . When I came to you, I did not come with eloquence or human wisdom as I proclaimed to you the testimony about God. For I resolved to know nothing while I was with you except Jesus Christ and him crucified. I came to you in weakness with great fear and trembling. My message and my preaching were not with wise and persuasive words, but with a demonstration of the Spirit's power, so that your faith might not rest on human wisdom, but on God's power.

1 CORINTHIANS 2:1–5

A Family Member Dies

He heals the brokenhearted
　　and binds up their wounds.
He determines the number of the stars
　　and calls them each by name.
Great is our Lord and mighty in power;
　　his understanding has no limit.

PSALM 147:3–5

Your kingdom is an everlasting kingdom,
　　and your dominion endures through all
　　　　generations.

The LORD is trustworthy in all he promises
　　and faithful in all he does.
The LORD upholds all who fall
　　and lifts up all who are bowed down.

PSALM 145:13–14

Brothers . . . we do not want you to be uninformed about those who sleep in death, so that you do not grieve like the rest of mankind, who have no hope. For we believe that Jesus died and rose again, and so we believe that God will bring with Jesus those who have fallen asleep in him. According to the Lord's word, we tell you that we who are still alive, who are left until the coming of the Lord, will certainly not precede those who have fallen asleep. For the Lord himself will come down from heaven, with a loud command, with the voice of the archangel and with the trumpet call of God, and the dead in Christ will rise first. After that, we who are still alive and are left will be caught up together with them in the clouds to meet the Lord in the air. And so we will be with the Lord forever. Therefore encourage one another with these words.

1 THESSALONIANS 4:13–18

For I am convinced that neither death nor life, neither angels nor demons, neither the present nor the future, nor any powers, neither height nor depth, nor anything else in all creation, will be able to separate us from the love of God that is in Christ Jesus our Lord.

ROMANS 8:38–39

For if the dead are not raised, then Christ has not been raised either. And if Christ has not been raised, your faith is futile; you are still in your sins. Then those also who have fallen asleep in Christ are lost. If only for this life we have hope in Christ, we are of all people most to be pitied.

But Christ has indeed been raised from the dead, the firstfruits of those who have fallen asleep. For since death came through a man, the resurrection of the dead comes also through a man. For as in Adam all die, so in Christ all will be made alive. But each in turn: Christ, the firstfruits; then, when he comes, those who belong to him. Then the end will come, when he hands over the kingdom to God the Father after he has destroyed all dominion, authority and power. For he must reign until he has put all his enemies under his feet. The last enemy to be destroyed is death. For he "has put everything under his feet." Now when it says that "everything" has been put under him, it is clear that this does not include God himself, who put everything under Christ. When he has done this, then the Son himself will be made subject to him who put everything under him, so that God may be all in all.

1 CORINTHIANS 15:16–28

There is a time for everything,
   and a season for every activity under the heavens:

a time to be born and a time to die,
a time to plant and a time to uproot,
a time to kill and a time to heal,
a time to tear down and a time to build,
a time to weep and a time to laugh,
a time to mourn and a time to dance,
a time to scatter stones and a time to gather
   them,
a time to embrace and a time to refrain from
   embracing,
a time to search and a time to give up,
a time to keep and a time to throw away,
a time to tear and a time to mend,
a time to be silent and a time to speak,
a time to love and a time to hate,
a time for war and a time for peace.

ECCLESIASTES 3:1–8

They Are Angry
and Need Peace

How good and pleasant it is
    when God's people live together in unity!

It is like precious oil poured on the head,
    running down on the beard,
running down on Aaron's beard,
    down on the collar of his robe.
It is as if the dew of Hermon
    were falling on Mount Zion.
For there the LORD bestows his blessing,
    even life forevermore.

PSALM 133:1–3

Whoever is patient has great understanding,
    but one who is quick-tempered displays folly.

PROVERBS 14:29

Better a small serving of vegetables with love
than a fattened calf with hatred.

A hot-tempered person stirs up conflict,
but the one who is patient calms a quarrel.

PROVERBS 15:17–18

My dear brothers . . . take note of this: Everyone
should be quick to listen, slow to speak and slow to
become angry, because human anger does not produce the righteousness that God desires.

JAMES 1:19–20

Better a patient person than a warrior,
one with self-control than one who takes a city.

PROVERBS 16:32

Starting a quarrel is like breaching a dam;
so drop the matter before a dispute breaks out.

PROVERBS 17:14

For God is not a God of disorder but of peace—as in
all the congregations of the Lord's people.

1 CORINTHIANS 14:33

"In your anger do not sin": Do not let the sun go down while you are still angry.

EPHESIANS 4:26

Let your conversation be always full of grace, seasoned with salt, so that you may know how to answer everyone.

COLOSSIANS 4:6

I appeal to you, brothers . . . in the name of our Lord Jesus Christ, that all of you agree with one another in what you say and that there be no divisions among you, but that you be perfectly united in mind and thought.

1 CORINTHIANS 1:10

Loved Ones Grow Apart

———◆———

So my spirit grows faint within me;
　　my heart within me is dismayed.
I remember the days of long ago;
　　I meditate on all your works
　　and consider what your hands have done.
I spread out my hands to you;
　　I thirst for you like a parched land.

Answer me quickly, LORD;
　　my spirit fails.
Do not hide your face from me
　　or I will be like those who go down to the pit.
Let the morning bring me word of your unfailing
　　　　love,
　　for I have put my trust in you.
Show me the way I should go,
　　for to you I entrust my life.

PSALM 143:4–8

Whoever gives heed to instruction prospers,
   and blessed is the one who trusts in the LORD.

The wise in heart are called discerning,
   and gracious words promote instruction.

PROVERBS 16:20–21

A happy heart makes the face cheerful,
   but heartache crushes the spirit.

The discerning heart seeks knowledge,
   but the mouth of a fool feeds on folly.

All the days of the oppressed are wretched,
   but the cheerful heart has a continual feast.

Better a little with the fear of the LORD
   than great wealth with turmoil.

PROVERBS 15:13–16

Jesus knew their thoughts and said to them, "Every kingdom divided against itself will be ruined, and every city or household divided against itself will not stand."

MATTHEW 12:25

A brother wronged is more unyielding than a
        fortified city;
    disputes are like the barred gates of a citadel.

Proverbs 18:19

A cheerful heart is good medicine,
    but a crushed spirit dries up the bones.

Proverbs 17:22

Better a dry crust with peace and quiet
    than a house full of feasting, with strife.

Proverbs 17:1

Make every effort to live in peace with everyone and
to be holy; without holiness no one will see the Lord.
See to it that no one falls short of the grace of God
and that no bitter root grows up to cause trouble and
defile many.

Hebrews 12:14–15

God

Challenges

Men *to* . . .

Grow in Their Christian Walk

———◆———

Teach me, LORD, the way of your decrees,
>that I may follow it to the end.
Give me understanding, so that I may keep your law
>and obey it with all my heart.
Direct me in the path of your commands,
>for there I find delight.

PSALM 119:33–35

We know that we have come to know him if we keep his commands. Whoever says, "I know him," but does not do what he commands is a liar, and the truth is not in that person. But if anyone obeys his word, love for God is truly made complete in them. This is how we know we are in him: Whoever claims to live in him must live as Jesus did.

1 JOHN 2:3–6

Therefore, since we have these promises, dear friends, let us purify ourselves from everything that contaminates body and spirit, perfecting holiness out of reverence for God.

2 CORINTHIANS 7:1

Your word is a lamp for my feet,
    a light on my path.
I have taken an oath and confirmed it,
    that I will follow your righteous laws.
I have suffered much;
    preserve my life, LORD, according to your word.
Accept, LORD, the willing praise of my mouth,
    and teach me your laws.
Though I constantly take my life in my hands,
    I will not forget your law.

PSALM 119:105–109

Apply your heart to instruction
    and your ears to words of knowledge.

PROVERBS 23:12

Fight the good fight of the faith. Take hold of the eternal life to which you were called when you made your good confession in the presence of many witnesses.

1 TIMOTHY 6:12

Those who live according to the flesh have their minds set on what the flesh desires; but those who live in accordance with the Spirit have their minds set on what the Spirit desires. The mind governed by the flesh is death, but the mind governed by the Spirit is life and peace.

ROMANS 8:5–6

And do this, understanding the present time: The hour has already come for you to wake up from your slumber, because our salvation is nearer now than when we first believed. The night is nearly over; the day is almost here. So let us put aside the deeds of darkness and put on the armor of light. Let us behave decently, as in the daytime, not in carousing and drunkenness, not in sexual immorality and debauchery, not in dissension and jealousy. Rather, clothe yourselves with the Lord Jesus Christ, and do not think about how to gratify the desires of the flesh.

ROMANS 13:11–14

Teach me your way, LORD,
    that I may rely on your faithfulness;
give me an undivided heart,
    that I may fear your name.
I will praise you, Lord my God, with all my heart;
    I will glorify your name forever.

PSALM 86:11–12

"Two men went up to the temple to pray, one a Pharisee and the other a tax collector. The Pharisee stood by himself and prayed: 'God, I thank you that I am not like other people—robbers, evildoers, adulterers—or even like this tax collector. I fast twice a week and give a tenth of all I get.'

"But the tax collector stood at a distance. He would not even look up to heaven, but beat his breast and said, 'God, have mercy on me, a sinner.'

"I tell you that this man, rather than the other, went home justified before God. For all those who exalt themselves will be humbled, and those who humble themselves will be exalted."

LUKE 18:10–14

Deal Honestly with Others

"Do not judge, or you too will be judged. For in the same way you judge others, you will be judged, and with the measure you use, it will be measured to you.

"Why do you look at the speck of sawdust in your brother's eye and pay no attention to the plank in your own eye? How can you say to your brother, 'Let me take the speck out of your eye,' when all the time there is a plank in your own eye? You hypocrite, first take the plank out of your own eye, and then you will see clearly to remove the speck from your brother's eye."

MATTHEW 7:1–5

Do not withhold good from those to whom it is due, when it is in your power to act.

PROVERBS 3:27

The LORD detests lying lips,
> but he delights in people who are trustworthy.

PROVERBS 12:22

The LORD sent Nathan to David. When he came to him, he said, "There were two men in a certain town, one rich and the other poor. The rich man had a very large number of sheep and cattle, but the poor man had nothing except one little ewe lamb he had bought. He raised it, and it grew up with him and his children. It shared his food, drank from his cup and even slept in his arms. It was like a daughter to him.

"Now a traveler came to the rich man, but the rich man refrained from taking one of his own sheep or cattle to prepare a meal for the traveler who had come to him. Instead, he took the ewe lamb that belonged to the poor man and prepared it for the one who had come to him."

David burned with anger against the man and said to Nathan, "As surely as the LORD lives, the man who did this must die! He must pay for that lamb four times over, because he did such a thing and had no pity."

Then Nathan said to David, "You are the man!"

2 SAMUEL 12:1–7

Do not lie to each other, since you have taken off your old self with its practices and have put on the new self, which is being renewed in knowledge in the image of its Creator. Here there is no Gentile or Jew, circumcised or uncircumcised, barbarian, Scythian, slave or free, but Christ is all, and is in all.

COLOSSIANS 3:9–11

Never take your word of truth from my mouth,
    for I have put my hope in your laws.
I will always obey your law,
    for ever and ever.
I will walk about in freedom,
    for I have sought out your precepts.

PSALM 119:43–45

You heard about Christ and were taught in him in accordance with the truth that is in Jesus. You were taught, with regard to your former way of life, to put off your old self, which is being corrupted by its deceitful desires; to be made new in the attitude of your minds; and to put on the new self, created to be like God in true righteousness and holiness.

EPHESIANS 4:21–24

Ask Forgiveness of Others

"So watch yourselves.

"If your brother or sister sins against you, rebuke them; and if they repent, forgive them. Even if they sin against you seven times in a day and seven times come back to you saying 'I repent,' you must forgive them."

LUKE 17:3–4

Pride brings a person low,
    but the lowly in spirit gain honor.

PROVERBS 29:23

"And when you stand praying, if you hold anything against anyone, forgive them, so that your Father in heaven may forgive you your sins."

MARK 11:25

As a prisoner for the Lord, then, I urge you to live a life worthy of the calling you have received. Be completely humble and gentle; be patient, bearing with one another in love. Make every effort to keep the unity of the Spirit through the bond of peace.

EPHESIANS 4:1–3

Bear with each other and forgive one another if any of you has a grievance against someone. Forgive as the Lord forgave you.

COLOSSIANS 3:13

"For if you forgive other people when they sin against you, your heavenly Father will also forgive you. But if you do not forgive others their sins, your Father will not forgive your sins."

MATTHEW 6:14–15

Get rid of all bitterness, rage and anger, brawling and slander, along with every form of malice. Be kind and compassionate to one another, forgiving each other, just as in Christ God forgave you.

EPHESIANS 4:31–32

Do not repay anyone evil for evil. Be careful to do what is right in the eyes of everyone. If it is possible, as far as it depends on you, live at peace with everyone. Do not take revenge, my dear friends, but leave room for God's wrath, for it is written: "It is mine to avenge; I will repay," says the Lord.

ROMANS 12:17–19

Whoever conceals their sins does not prosper,
　　but the one who confesses and renounces them
　　　　finds mercy.

PROVERBS 28:13

Share Their Faith with Others

———◆———

But what does it say? "The word is near you; it is in your mouth and in your heart," that is, the message concerning faith that we proclaim: If you declare with your mouth, "Jesus is Lord," and believe in your heart that God raised him from the dead, you will be saved. For it is with your heart that you believe and are justified, and it is with your mouth that you profess your faith and are saved. As Scripture says, "Anyone who believes in him will never be put to shame."

ROMANS 10:8–11

"His master replied, 'Well done, good and faithful servant! You have been faithful with a few things; I will put you in charge of many things. Come and share your master's happiness!'"

MATTHEW 25:21

So Christ himself gave the apostles, the prophets, the evangelists, the pastors and teachers, to equip his people for works of service, so that the body of Christ may be built up until we all reach unity in the faith and in the knowledge of the Son of God and become mature, attaining to the whole measure of the fullness of Christ.

Then we will no longer be infants, tossed back and forth by the waves, and blown here and there by every wind of teaching and by the cunning and craftiness of people in their deceitful scheming. Instead, speaking the truth in love, we will grow to become in every respect the mature body of him who is the head, that is, Christ.

EPHESIANS 4:11–15

My brothers . . . if one of you should wander from the truth and someone should bring that person back, remember this: Whoever turns a sinner from the error of their way will save them from death and cover over a multitude of sins.

JAMES 5:19–20

"Very truly I tell you, whoever believes in me will do the works I have been doing, and they will do even greater things than these, because I am going to the Father. And I will do whatever you ask in my name, so that the Father may be glorified in the Son."

JOHN 14:12–13

Let us not become weary in doing good, for at the proper time we will reap a harvest if we do not give up. Therefore, as we have opportunity, let us do good to all people, especially to those who belong to the family of believers.

GALATIANS 6:9–10

Let your conversation be always full of grace, seasoned with salt, so that you may know how to answer everyone.

COLOSSIANS 4:6

Always be prepared to give an answer to everyone who asks you to give the reason for the hope that you have. But do this with gentleness and respect.

1 PETER 3:15

I am not ashamed of the gospel, because it is the power of God that brings salvation to everyone who believes.

ROMANS 1:16

God . . . reconciled us to himself through Christ and gave us the ministry of reconciliation: that God was reconciling the world to himself in Christ, not counting people's sins against them. And he has committed to us the message of reconciliation. We are therefore Christ's ambassadors, as though God were making his appeal through us.

2 CORINTHIANS 5:18–20

Be Wise with Their Finances

—◆—

Trust in the LORD and do good;
    dwell in the land and enjoy safe pasture.
Take delight in the LORD,
    and he will give you the desires of your heart.

Commit your way to the LORD;
    trust in him and he will do this.
He will make your righteous reward shine like
      the dawn,
    your vindication like the noonday sun.

PSALM 37:3–5

But remember the LORD your God, for it is he who gives you the ability to produce wealth, and so confirms his covenant, which he swore to your ancestors, as it is today.

DEUTERONOMY 8:18

If you fully obey the LORD your God and carefully follow all his commands I give you today, the LORD your God will set you high above all the nations on earth. All these blessings will come on you and accompany you if you obey the LORD your God:

> You will be blessed in the city and blessed in the country.

> The fruit of your womb will be blessed, and the crops of your land and the young of your livestock—the calves of your herds and the lambs of your flocks.

> Your basket and your kneading trough will be blessed.

> You will be blessed when you come in and blessed when you go out.

DEUTERONOMY 28:1–6

Whoever puts up security for a stranger will
    surely suffer,
  but whoever refuses to shake hands in pledge
    is safe.

PROVERBS 11:15

"Do not store up for yourselves treasures on earth, where moths and vermin destroy, and where thieves break in and steal. But store up for yourselves treasures in heaven, where moths and vermin do not destroy, and where thieves do not break in and steal. For where your treasure is, there your heart will be also."

MATTHEW 6:19–21

The LORD sends poverty and wealth;
    he humbles and he exalts.
He raises the poor from the dust
    and lifts the needy from the ash heap;
he seats them with princes
    and has them inherit a throne of honor.

For the foundations of the earth are the LORD's;
    on them he has set the world.
He will guard the feet of his faithful servants,
    but the wicked will be silenced in the place of
        darkness.

It is not by strength that one prevails.

1 SAMUEL 2:7–9

Be Accountable to Christian Brothers

⊷◆⊶

Two are better than one,
  because they have a good return for their labor:
If either of them falls down,
  one can help the other up.
But pity anyone who falls
  and has no one to help them up.

ECCLESIASTES 4:9–10

Be devoted to one another in love. Honor one another above yourselves.

ROMANS 12:10

One who has unreliable friends soon comes to ruin,
  but there is a friend who sticks closer than a
    brother.

PROVERBS 18:24

As iron sharpens iron,

> so one person sharpens another.

Proverbs 27:17

Therefore confess your sins to each other and pray for each other so that you may be healed. The prayer of a righteous person is powerful and effective.

James 5:16

Our presentable parts need no special treatment. But God has put the body together, giving greater honor to the parts that lacked it, so that there should be no division in the body, but that its parts should have equal concern for each other. If one part suffers, every part suffers with it; if one part is honored, every part rejoices with it.

1 Corinthians 12:24–26

For now we see only a reflection as in a mirror; then we shall see face to face. Now I know in part; then I shall know fully, even as I am fully known.

1 Corinthians 13:12

"Remain in me, as I also remain in you. No branch can bear fruit by itself; it must remain in the vine. Neither can you bear fruit unless you remain in me.

"I am the vine; you are the branches. If you remain in me and I in you, you will bear much fruit; apart from me you can do nothing."

JOHN 15:4–5

Now that you have purified yourselves by obeying the truth so that you have sincere love for each other, love one another deeply, from the heart.

1 PETER 1:22

"A new command I give you: Love one another. As I have loved you, so you must love one another."

JOHN 13:34

As a prisoner for the Lord, then, I urge you to live a life worthy of the calling you have received. Be completely humble and gentle; be patient, bearing with one another in love. Make every effort to keep the unity of the Spirit through the bond of peace.

EPHESIANS 4:1–3

Do nothing out of selfish ambition or vain conceit. Rather, in humility value others above yourselves, not looking to your own interests but each of you to the interests of the others.

PHILIPPIANS 2:3–4

My brothers . . . if one of you should wander from the truth and someone should bring that person back, remember this: Whoever turns a sinner from the error of their way will save them from death and cover over a multitude of sins.

JAMES 5:19–20

Brothers . . . if someone is caught in a sin, you who live by the Spirit should restore that person gently. But watch yourselves, or you also may be tempted.

GALATIANS 6:1

Finally, all of you, be like-minded, be sympathetic, love one another, be compassionate and humble. Do not repay evil with evil or insult with insult. On the contrary, repay evil with blessing, because to this you were called so that you may inherit a blessing.

1 PETER 3:8–9

God Listens *to*
Men's Prayers
When . . .

No One Else Will Listen

"Ask and it will be given to you; seek and you will find; knock and the door will be opened to you. For everyone who asks receives; the one who seeks finds; and to the one who knocks, the door will be opened."

MATTHEW 7:7–8

Devote yourselves to prayer, being watchful and thankful.

COLOSSIANS 4:2

Be joyful in hope, patient in affliction, faithful in prayer. Share with the Lord's people who are in need. Practice hospitality.

ROMANS 12:12–13

Rejoice always, pray continually, give thanks in all circumstances; for this is God's will for you in Christ Jesus.

1 THESSALONIANS 5:16–18

"If my people, who are called by my name, will humble themselves and pray and seek my face and turn from their wicked ways, then I will hear from heaven, and I will forgive their sin and will heal their land."

2 CHRONICLES 7:14

Therefore put on the full armor of God, so that when the day of evil comes, you may be able to stand your ground, and after you have done everything, to stand. Stand firm then, with the belt of truth buckled around your waist, with the breastplate of righteousness in place, and with your feet fitted with the readiness that comes from the gospel of peace. In addition to all this, take up the shield of faith, with which you can extinguish all the flaming arrows of the evil one. Take the helmet of salvation and the sword of the Spirit, which is the word of God.

And pray in the Spirit on all occasions with all kinds of prayers and requests. With this in mind, be alert and always keep on praying for all the Lord's people.

EPHESIANS 6:13–18

"Again, truly I tell you that if two of you on earth agree about anything they ask for, it will be done for them by my Father in heaven. For where two or three gather in my name, there am I with them."

MATTHEW 18:19–20

Hear me, LORD, my plea is just;
     listen to my cry.
Hear my prayer—
     it does not rise from deceitful lips.

PSALM 17:1

For the eyes of the Lord are on the righteous
     and his ears are attentive to their prayer,
but the face of the Lord is against those who do evil."

1 PETER 3:12

Answer me when I call to you,
     my righteous God.
Give me relief from my distress;
     have mercy on me and hear my prayer.

PSALM 4:1

Let us then approach God's throne of grace with confidence, so that we may receive mercy and find grace
to help us in our time of need.

HEBREWS 4:16

"So I say to you: Ask and it will be given to you; seek
and you will find; knock and the door will be opened
to you."

LUKE 11:9

They Ask for Patience

Consider it pure joy, my brothers . . . whenever you face trials of many kinds, because you know that the testing of your faith produces perseverance. Let perseverance finish its work so that you may be mature and complete, not lacking anything.

JAMES 1:2–4

And the Lord's servant must not be quarrelsome but must be kind to everyone, able to teach, not resentful.

2 TIMOTHY 2:24

Therefore, since we are surrounded by such a great cloud of witnesses, let us throw off everything that hinders and the sin that so easily entangles. And let us run with perseverance the race marked out for us.

HEBREWS 12:1

For even Christ did not please himself but, as it is written: "The insults of those who insult you have fallen on me." For everything that was written in the past was written to teach us, so that through the endurance taught in the Scriptures and the encouragement they provide we might have hope.

May the God who gives endurance and encouragement give you the same attitude of mind toward each other that Christ Jesus had.

ROMANS 15:3–5

Therefore if you have any encouragement from being united with Christ, if any comfort from his love, if any common sharing in the Spirit, if any tenderness and compassion, then make my joy complete by being like-minded, having the same love, being one in spirit and of one mind. Do nothing out of selfish ambition or vain conceit. Rather, in humility value others above yourselves, not looking to your own interests but each of you to the interests of the others.

PHILIPPIANS 2:1–4

Wait for the LORD;
> be strong and take heart
> and wait for the LORD.

PSALM 27:14

Be still before the LORD
> and wait patiently for him;
do not fret when people succeed in their ways,
> when they carry out their wicked schemes.

Refrain from anger and turn from wrath;
> do not fret—it leads only to evil.
For those who are evil will be destroyed,
> but those who hope in the LORD will inherit the
> > land.

PSALM 37:7–9

The end of a matter is better than its beginning,
> and patience is better than pride.
Do not be quickly provoked in your spirit,
> for anger resides in the lap of fools.

ECCLESIASTES 7:8–9

They Ask for Guidance from the Holy Spirit

—◆—

Teach me to do your will,
for you are my God;
may your good Spirit
lead me on level ground.

For your name's sake, LORD, preserve my life;
in your righteousness, bring me out of trouble.

PSALM 143:10–11

Now the Lord is the Spirit, and where the Spirit of the Lord is, there is freedom. And we all, who with unveiled faces contemplate the Lord's glory, are being transformed into his image with ever-increasing glory, which comes from the Lord, who is the Spirit.

2 CORINTHIANS 3:17–18

So I say, walk by the Spirit, and you will not gratify the desires of the flesh. For the flesh desires what is contrary to the Spirit, and the Spirit what is contrary to the flesh. They are in conflict with each other, so that you are not to do whatever you want. But if you are led by the Spirit, you are not under the law.

The acts of the flesh are obvious: sexual immorality, impurity and debauchery; idolatry and witchcraft; hatred, discord, jealousy, fits of rage, selfish ambition, dissensions, factions and envy; drunkenness, orgies, and the like. I warn you, as I did before, that those who live like this will not inherit the kingdom of God.

But the fruit of the Spirit is love, joy, peace, forbearance, kindness, goodness, faithfulness, gentleness and self-control. Against such things there is no law. Those who belong to Christ Jesus have crucified the flesh with its passions and desires. Since we live by the Spirit, let us keep in step with the Spirit. Let us not become conceited, provoking and envying each other.

GALATIANS 5:16–26

These are the things God has revealed to us by his Spirit.

The Spirit searches all things, even the deep things of God. For who knows a person's thoughts except their own spirit within them? In the same way no one knows the thoughts of God except the Spirit of God. What we have received is not the spirit of the world, but the Spirit who is from God, so that we may understand what God has freely given us. This is what we speak, not in words taught us by human wisdom but in words taught by the Spirit, explaining spiritual realities with Spirit-taught words. The person without the Spirit does not accept the things that come from the Spirit of God but considers them foolishness, and cannot understand them because they are discerned only through the Spirit. The person with the Spirit makes judgments about all things, but such a person is not subject to merely human judgments, for,

"Who has known the mind of the Lord
    so as to instruct him?"

But we have the mind of Christ.

1 Corinthians 2:10–16

"And I will ask the Father, and he will give you another advocate to help you and be with you forever—the Spirit of truth. The world cannot accept him, because it neither sees him nor knows him. But you know him, for he lives with you and will be in you."

JOHN 14:16–17

"But very truly I tell you, it is for your good that I am going away. Unless I go away, the Advocate will not come to you; but if I go, I will send him to you. When he comes, he will prove the world to be in the wrong about sin and righteousness and judgment. . . .

"But when he, the Spirit of truth, comes, he will guide you into all the truth. He will not speak on his own; he will speak only what he hears, and he will tell you what is yet to come. He will glorify me because it is from me that he will receive what he will make known to you. All that belongs to the Father is mine. That is why I said the Spirit will receive from me what he will make known to you."

JOHN 16:7–8, 13–15

They Confess Their Sins and Seek Forgiveness

The LORD is far from the wicked,
> but he hears the prayer of the righteous.

Light in a messenger's eyes brings joy to the heart,
> and good news gives health to the bones.

Whoever heeds life-giving correction
> will be at home among the wise.

Those who disregard discipline despise themselves,
> but the one who heeds correction gains
> > understanding.

Wisdom's instruction is to fear the LORD,
> and humility comes before honor.

PROVERBS 15:29–33

Whoever conceals their sins does not prosper,
>	but the one who confesses and renounces them
>>		finds mercy.

PROVERBS 28:13

If we confess our sins, he is faithful and just and will forgive us our sins and purify us from all unrighteousness.

1 JOHN 1:9

"This is the covenant I will establish with the people
>		of Israel
>	after that time, declares the Lord.

I will put my laws in their minds
>	and write them on their hearts.

I will be their God,
>	and they will be my people.

No longer will they teach their neighbor,
>	or say to one another, 'Know the Lord,'

because they will all know me,
>	from the least of them to the greatest.

For I will forgive their wickedness
>	and will remember their sins no more."

HEBREWS 8:10–12

Let the wicked forsake their ways
    and the unrighteous their thoughts.
Let them turn to the Lord, and he will have mercy
      on them,
    and to our God, for he will freely pardon.

Isaiah 55:7

To the praise of his glorious grace, which he has freely given us in the One he loves. In him we have redemption through his blood, the forgiveness of sins, in accordance with the riches of God's grace.

Ephesians 1:6–7

"Come now, let us settle the matter,"
    says the Lord.
"Though your sins are like scarlet,
    they shall be as white as snow;
though they are red as crimson,
    they shall be like wool.
If you are willing and obedient,
    you will eat the good things of the land."

Isaiah 1:18–19

Blessed is the one
>	whose transgressions are forgiven,
>	whose sins are covered.

Blessed is the one
>	whose sin the LORD does not count against them
>	and in whose spirit is no deceit.

PSALM 32:1–2

My dear children, I write this to you so that you will not sin. But if anybody does sin, we have an advocate with the Father—Jesus Christ, the Righteous One.

1 JOHN 2:1

The Responsibilities of Life Are Overwhelming

———◆———

"Though the mountains be shaken
    and the hills be removed,
yet my unfailing love for you will not be shaken
    nor my covenant of peace be removed,"
        says the LORD, who has compassion on you.

ISAIAH 54:10

So then, brothers . . . stand firm and hold fast to the teachings we passed on to you, whether by word of mouth or by letter.

May our Lord Jesus Christ himself and God our Father, who loved us and by his grace gave us eternal encouragement and good hope, encourage your hearts and strengthen you in every good deed and word.

2 THESSALONIANS 2:15–17

"Be strong and courageous. Do not be afraid or terrified because of them, for the LORD your God goes with you; he will never leave you nor forsake you."

DEUTERONOMY 31:6

Unless the LORD builds the house,
　　the builders labor in vain.
Unless the LORD watches over the city,
　　the guards stand watch in vain.
In vain you rise early
　　and stay up late,
toiling for food to eat—
　　for he grants sleep to those he loves.

Children are a heritage from the LORD,
　　offspring a reward from him.
Like arrows in the hands of a warrior
　　are children born in one's youth.
Blessed is the man
　　whose quiver is full of them.
They will not be put to shame
　　when they contend with their opponents in
　　　　court.

PSALM 127:1–5

Lift up your eyes and look to the heavens:
Who created all these?
He who brings out the starry host one by one
and calls forth each of them by name.
Because of his great power and mighty strength,
not one of them is missing.

Why do you complain, Jacob?
Why do you say, Israel,
"My way is hidden from the LORD;
my cause is disregarded by my God"?
Do you not know?
Have you not heard?
The LORD is the everlasting God,
the Creator of the ends of the earth.
He will not grow tired or weary,
and his understanding no one can fathom.
He gives strength to the weary
and increases the power of the weak.

ISAIAH 40:26–29

"For I know the plans I have for you," declares the LORD, "plans to prosper you and not to harm you, plans to give you hope and a future. Then you will call on me and come and pray to me, and I will listen to you. You will seek me and find me when you seek me with all your heart."

JEREMIAH 29:11–13

"Do not be afraid, for I am with you;
    I will bring your children from the east
    and gather you from the west.
I will say to the north, 'Give them up!'
    and to the south, 'Do not hold them back.'
Bring my sons from afar
    and my daughters from the ends of the earth—
everyone who is called by my name,
    whom I created for my glory,
    whom I formed and made."

ISAIAH 43:5–7

God Fills

Men *with* Joy

When . . .

They Praise the Lord

I thank and praise you, God of my ancestors:
    You have given me wisdom and power,
you have made known to me what we asked of you,
    you have made known to us the dream of
        the king.

DANIEL 2:23

Young men and women,
    old men and children.

Let them praise the name of the LORD,
    for his name alone is exalted;
        his splendor is above the earth and the heavens.
And he has raised up for his people a horn,
    the praise of all his faithful servants,
        of Israel, the people close to his heart.

Praise the LORD.

PSALM 148:12–14

I will exalt you, my God the King;
    I will praise your name for ever and ever.
Every day I will praise you
    and extol your name for ever and ever.

Great is the LORD and most worthy of praise;
    his greatness no one can fathom.
One generation commends your works to another;
    they tell of your mighty acts.

PSALM 145:1–4

"I provide water in the wilderness
    and streams in the wasteland,
to give drink to my people, my chosen,
    the people I formed for myself
    that they may proclaim my praise."

ISAIAH 43:20–21

But you are a chosen people, a royal priesthood, a holy
nation, God's special possession, that you may declare
the praises of him who called you out of darkness into
his wonderful light.

1 PETER 2:9

Praise the LORD.

Praise God in his sanctuary;
  praise him in his mighty heavens.
Praise him for his acts of power;
  praise him for his surpassing greatness.
Praise him with the sounding of the trumpet,
  praise him with the harp and lyre,
praise him with timbrel and dancing,
  praise him with the strings and pipe,
praise him with the clash of cymbals,
  praise him with resounding cymbals.
Let everything that has breath praise the LORD.
Praise the LORD.

PSALM 150:1–6

Know that the LORD is God.
  It is he who made us, and we are his;
  we are his people, the sheep of his pasture.

Enter his gates with thanksgiving
  and his courts with praise;
  give thanks to him and praise his name.
For the LORD is good and his love endures forever;
  his faithfulness continues through all generations.

PSALM 100:3–5

They Worship God

Ascribe to the LORD the glory due his name;
  bring an offering and come before him.
Worship the LORD in the splendor of his
          holiness. . . .

Let the heavens rejoice, let the earth be glad;
  let them say among the nations, "The LORD
          reigns!"
Let the sea resound, and all that is in it;
  let the fields be jubilant, and everything in them!
Let the trees of the forest sing,
  let them sing for joy before the LORD,
  for he comes to judge the earth.

                                    1 CHRONICLES 16:29, 31–33

Jesus said to him, "Away from me, Satan! For it is
written: 'Worship the Lord your God, and serve him
only.'"

                                    MATTHEW 4:10

Come, let us bow down in worship,
    let us kneel before the LORD our Maker;
for he is our God
    and we are the people of his pasture,
    the flock under his care.

PSALM 95:6–7

"Yet a time is coming and has now come when the true worshipers will worship the Father in the Spirit and in truth, for they are the kind of worshipers the Father seeks. God is spirit, and his worshipers must worship in the Spirit and in truth."

JOHN 4:23–24

Shout for joy to the LORD, all the earth.
    Worship the LORD with gladness;
    come before him with joyful songs.

PSALM 100:1–2

"The LORD lives! Praise be to my Rock!
    Exalted be my God, the Rock, my Savior!"

2 SAMUEL 22:47

Whenever the living creatures give glory, honor and thanks to him who sits on the throne and who lives for ever and ever, the twenty-four elders fall down before him who sits on the throne and worship him who lives for ever and ever. They lay their crowns before the throne and say:

> "You are worthy, our Lord and God,
>   to receive glory and honor and power,
> for you created all things,
>   and by your will they were created
>   and have their being."

REVELATION 4:9–11

Then I saw another angel flying in midair, and he had the eternal gospel to proclaim to those who live on the earth—to every nation, tribe, language and people. He said in a loud voice, "Fear God and give him glory, because the hour of his judgment has come. Worship him who made the heavens, the earth, the sea and the springs of water."

REVELATION 14:6–7

Their Children Grow to Love the Lord

——◆——

I love those who love me,
  and those who seek me find me. . . .
Bestowing a rich inheritance on those who love me
  and making their treasuries full.

PROVERBS 8:17, 21

Christ may dwell in your hearts through faith. And I pray that you, being rooted and established in love, may have power, together with all the Lord's holy people, to grasp how wide and long and high and deep is the love of Christ, and to know this love that surpasses knowledge—that you may be filled to the measure of all the fullness of God.

EPHESIANS 3:17–19

"You are the salt of the earth. But if the salt loses its saltiness, how can it be made salty again? It is no longer good for anything, except to be thrown out and trampled underfoot.

"You are the light of the world. A town built on a hill cannot be hidden. Neither do people light a lamp and put it under a bowl. Instead they put it on its stand, and it gives light to everyone in the house. In the same way, let your light shine before others, that they may see your good deeds and glorify your Father in heaven."

MATTHEW 5:13–16

"As the Father has loved me, so have I loved you. Now remain in my love. If you keep my commands, you will remain in my love, just as I have kept my Father's commands and remain in his love. I have told you this so that my joy may be in you and that your joy may be complete. My command is this: Love each other as I have loved you."

JOHN 15:9–12

"'Love the Lord your God with all your heart and with all your soul and with all your mind and with all your strength.' The second is this: 'Love your neighbor as yourself.' There is no commandment greater than these."

Mark 12:30–31

But be very careful to keep the commandment and the law that Moses the servant of the Lord gave you: to love the Lord your God, to walk in obedience to him, to keep his commands, to hold fast to him and to serve him with all your heart and with all your soul.

Joshua 22:5

Jesus replied: "'Love the Lord your God with all your heart and with all your soul and with all your mind.' This is the first and greatest commandment. And the second is like it: 'Love your neighbor as yourself.' All the Law and the Prophets hang on these two commandments."

Matthew 22:37–40

God Keeps
Men Secure
When . . .

They Put God First in Their Lives

———◆———

Humble yourselves, therefore, under God's mighty hand, that he may lift you up in due time. Cast all your anxiety on him because he cares for you.

1 PETER 5:6–7

My son, if you accept my words
    and store up my commands within you,
turning your ear to wisdom
    and applying your heart to understanding—
indeed, if you call out for insight
    and cry aloud for understanding,
and if you look for it as for silver
    and search for it as for hidden treasure,
then you will understand the fear of the LORD
    and find the knowledge of God.

PROVERBS 2:1–5

Be strong and courageous. Do not be afraid or terrified because of them, for the LORD your God goes with you; he will never leave you nor forsake you.

DEUTERONOMY 31:6

I love you, LORD, my strength.

The LORD is my rock, my fortress and my deliverer;
    my God is my rock, in whom I take refuge,
    my shield and the horn of my salvation, my
        stronghold.

I called to the LORD, who is worthy of praise,
    and I have been saved from my enemies. . . .

They confronted me in the day of my disaster,
    but the LORD was my support.

PSALM 18:1–3, 18

Submit yourselves, then, to God. Resist the devil, and he will flee from you. Come near to God and he will come near to you. Wash your hands, you sinners, and purify your hearts, you double-minded.

JAMES 4:7–8

"Keep this Book of the Law always on your lips; meditate on it day and night, so that you may be careful to do everything written in it. Then you will be prosperous and successful. Have I not commanded you? Be strong and courageous. Do not be afraid; do not be discouraged, for the LORD your God will be with you wherever you go."

JOSHUA 1:8–9

For wisdom will enter your heart,
    and knowledge will be pleasant to your soul.
Discretion will protect you,
    and understanding will guard you.

Wisdom will save you from the ways of wicked men,
    from men whose words are perverse.

PROVERBS 2:10–12

They Make a Major Job Change

———◆———

What do workers gain from their toil? I have seen the burden God has laid on the human race. He has made everything beautiful in its time. He has also set eternity in the human heart; yet no one can fathom what God has done from beginning to end. I know that there is nothing better for people than to be happy and to do good while they live. That each of them may eat and drink, and find satisfaction in all their toil—this is the gift of God.

ECCLESIASTES 3:9–13

Therefore, my dear brothers . . . stand firm. Let nothing move you. Always give yourselves fully to the work of the Lord, because you know that your labor in the Lord is not in vain.

1 CORINTHIANS 15:58

I hated all the things I had toiled for under the sun, because I must leave them to the one who comes after me. And who knows whether that person will be wise or foolish? Yet they will have control over all the fruit of my toil into which I have poured my effort and skill under the sun. This too is meaningless. So my heart began to despair over all my toilsome labor under the sun. For a person may labor with wisdom, knowledge and skill, and then they must leave all they own to another who has not toiled for it. This too is meaningless and a great misfortune. What do people get for all the toil and anxious striving with which they labor under the sun? All their days their work is grief and pain; even at night their minds do not rest. This too is meaningless.

A person can do nothing better than to eat and drink and find satisfaction in their own toil. This too, I see, is from the hand of God, for without him, who can eat or find enjoyment? To the person who pleases him, God gives wisdom, knowledge and happiness, but to the sinner he gives the task of gathering and storing up wealth to hand it over to the one who pleases God. This too is meaningless, a chasing after the wind.

ECCLESIASTES 2:18–26

For no one can lay any foundation other than the one already laid, which is Jesus Christ. If anyone builds on this foundation using gold, silver, costly stones, wood, hay or straw, their work will be shown for what it is, because the Day will bring it to light. It will be revealed with fire, and the fire will test the quality of each person's work. If what has been built survives, the builder will receive a reward. If it is burned up, the builder will suffer loss but yet will be saved—even though only as one escaping through the flames.

1 CORINTHIANS 3:11–15

Do not wear yourself out to get rich;
> do not trust your own cleverness.
Cast but a glance at riches, and they are gone,
> for they will surely sprout wings
> and fly off to the sky like an eagle.

PROVERBS 23:4–5

But whoever looks intently into the perfect law that gives freedom, and continues in it—not forgetting what they have heard, but doing it—they will be blessed in what they do.

JAMES 1:25

"Therefore I tell you, do not worry about your life, what you will eat or drink; or about your body, what you will wear. Is not life more than food, and the body more than clothes? Look at the birds of the air; they do not sow or reap or store away in barns, and yet your heavenly Father feeds them. Are you not much more valuable than they? Can any one of you by worrying add a single hour to your life?

"And why do you worry about clothes? See how the flowers of the field grow. They do not labor or spin. Yet I tell you that not even Solomon in all his splendor was dressed like one of these. If that is how God clothes the grass of the field, which is here today and tomorrow is thrown into the fire, will he not much more clothe you—you of little faith? So do not worry, saying, 'What shall we eat?' or 'What shall we drink?' or 'What shall we wear?' For the pagans run after all these things, and your heavenly Father knows that you need them. But seek first his kingdom and his righteousness, and all these things will be given to you as well. Therefore do not worry about tomorrow, for tomorrow will worry about itself. Each day has enough trouble of its own."

MATTHEW 6:25–34

The name of the LORD is a fortified tower;
    the righteous run to it and are safe.

PROVERBS 18:10

Do not put your trust in princes,
    in human beings, who cannot save.
When their spirit departs, they return to the ground;
    on that very day their plans come to nothing.
Blessed are those whose help is the God of Jacob,
    whose hope is in the LORD their God.

PSALM 146:3–5

Worry and Doubt Threaten Their Well-Being

——◆——

You will keep in perfect peace
    those whose minds are steadfast,
    because they trust in you.

ISAIAH 26:3

The fruit of that righteousness will be peace;
    its effect will be quietness and confidence
        forever.
My people will live in peaceful dwelling places,
    in secure homes,
    in undisturbed places of rest.

ISAIAH 32:17–18

The eyes of all look to you,
and you give them their food at the proper time.
You open your hand
and satisfy the desires of every living thing.

The LORD is righteous in all his ways
and faithful in all he does.
The LORD is near to all who call on him,
to all who call on him in truth.
He fulfills the desires of those who fear him;
he hears their cry and saves them.
The LORD watches over all who love him,
but all the wicked he will destroy.

My mouth will speak in praise of the LORD.
Let every creature praise his holy name
for ever and ever.

PSALM 145:15–21

In peace I will lie down and sleep,
for you alone, LORD,
make me dwell in safety.

PSALM 4:8

Blessed are all who fear the LORD,
  who walk in obedience to him.
You will eat the fruit of your labor;
  blessings and prosperity will be yours.
Your wife will be like a fruitful vine
  within your house;
your children will be like olive shoots
  around your table.
Yes, this will be the blessing
  for the man who fears the LORD.

May the LORD bless you from Zion;
  may you see the prosperity of Jerusalem
  all the days of your life.
May you live to see your children's children—
  peace be on Israel.

PSALM 128:1–6

For I will pour water on the thirsty land,
  and streams on the dry ground;
I will pour out my Spirit on your offspring,
  and my blessing on your descendants.

ISAIAH 44:3

But it was because the LORD loved you and kept the oath he swore to your ancestors that he brought you out with a mighty hand and redeemed you from the land of slavery, from the power of Pharaoh king of Egypt. Know therefore that the LORD your God is God; he is the faithful God, keeping his covenant of love to a thousand generations of those who love him and keep his commandments.

DEUTERONOMY 7:8–9

Your love, LORD, reaches to the heavens,
    your faithfulness to the skies.

PSALM 36:5

Praise be to the Lord, to God our Savior,
    who daily bears our burdens.

PSALM 68:19

They Don't Have Money to Pay the Bills

—◆—

The lions may grow weak and hungry,
    but those who seek the LORD lack no good thing.
PSALM 34:10

The poor will see and be glad—
    you who seek God, may your hearts live!
The LORD hears the needy
    and does not despise his captive people.
PSALM 69:32–33

The LORD will send a blessing on your barns and on everything you put your hand to. The LORD your God will bless you in the land he is giving you.
DEUTERONOMY 28:8

I was young and now I am old,
    yet I have never seen the righteous forsaken
    or their children begging bread.
They are always generous and lend freely;
    their children will be a blessing.

Turn from evil and do good;
    then you will dwell in the land forever.
For the LORD loves the just
    and will not forsake his faithful ones.

Wrongdoers will be completely destroyed;
    the offspring of the wicked will perish.

PSALM 37:25–28

You will have plenty to eat, until you are full,
    and you will praise the name of the LORD your
        God,
    who has worked wonders for you;
never again will my people be shamed.
Then you will know that I am in Israel,
    that I am the LORD your God,
    and that there is no other;
never again will my people be shamed.

JOEL 2:26–27

"The poor and needy search for water,
　　but there is none;
　　their tongues are parched with thirst.
But I the Lord will answer them;
　　I, the God of Israel, will not forsake them."

ISAIAH 41:17

And my God will meet all your needs according to
the riches of his glory in Christ Jesus.

PHILIPPIANS 4:19

"I will satisfy the priests with abundance,
　　and my people will be filled with my bounty,"
　　declares the Lord.

JEREMIAH 31:14

God Comforts

Men When . . .

They Feel Inadequate for Their Responsibilities

———◆———

"Come to me, all you who are weary and burdened, and I will give you rest. Take my yoke upon you and learn from me, for I am gentle and humble in heart, and you will find rest for your souls. For my yoke is easy and my burden is light."

MATTHEW 11:28–30

For the eyes of the LORD range throughout the earth to strengthen those whose hearts are fully committed to him.

2 CHRONICLES 16:9

"I will be a Father to you,
    and you will be my sons and daughters,
    says the Lord Almighty."

2 CORINTHIANS 6:18

Not that we are competent in ourselves to claim anything for ourselves, but our competence comes from God.

2 Corinthians 3:5

My heart is not proud, Lord,
　　my eyes are not haughty;
I do not concern myself with great matters
　　or things too wonderful for me.
But I have calmed and quieted myself,
　　I am like a weaned child with its mother;
　　like a weaned child I am content.

Israel, put your hope in the Lord
　　both now and forevermore.

Psalm 131:1–3

But by the grace of God I am what I am, and his grace to me was not without effect. No, I worked harder than all of them—yet not I, but the grace of God that was with me. Whether, then, it is I or they, this is what we preach, and this is what you believed.

1 Corinthians 15:10–11

"I have swept away your offenses like a cloud,
　　your sins like the morning mist.
Return to me,
　　for I have redeemed you."

Isaiah 44:22

Through these he has given us his very great and precious promises, so that through them you may participate in the divine nature, having escaped the corruption in the world caused by evil desires.

For this very reason, make every effort to add to your faith goodness; and to goodness, knowledge; and to knowledge, self-control; and to self-control, perseverance; and to perseverance, godliness; and to godliness, mutual affection; and to mutual affection, love. For if you possess these qualities in increasing measure, they will keep you from being ineffective and unproductive in your knowledge of our Lord Jesus Christ.

2 Peter 1:4–8

Their Loved Ones Are Ill

—◆—

Dear friend, I pray that you may enjoy good health and that all may go well with you, even as your soul is getting along well. It gave me great joy when some believers came and testified about your faithfulness to the truth, telling how you continue to walk in it. I have no greater joy than to hear that my children are walking in the truth.

3 John vv. 2–4

"'If you can'?" said Jesus. "Everything is possible for one who believes."

Immediately the boy's father exclaimed, "I do believe; help me overcome my unbelief!"

Mark 9:23–24

But he was pierced for our transgressions,
    he was crushed for our iniquities;
the punishment that brought us peace was on him,
    and by his wounds we are healed.

Isaiah 53:5

When Jesus entered the synagogue leader's house and saw the noisy crowd and people playing pipes, he said, "Go away. The girl is not dead but asleep." But they laughed at him. After the crowd had been put outside, he went in and took the girl by the hand, and she got up. News of this spread through all that region.

Matthew 9:23–26

Is anyone among you sick? Let them call the elders of the church to pray over them and anoint them with oil in the name of the Lord. And the prayer offered in faith will make the sick person well; the Lord will raise them up. If they have sinned, they will be forgiven. Therefore confess your sins to each other and pray for each other so that you may be healed. The prayer of a righteous person is powerful and effective.

James 5:14–16

"He himself bore our sins" in his body on the cross, so that we might die to sins and live for righteousness; "by his wounds you have been healed."

1 PETER 2:24

Heal me, LORD, and I will be healed;
    save me and I will be saved,
    for you are the one I praise.

JEREMIAH 17:14

He said, "If you listen carefully to the LORD your God and do what is right in his eyes, if you pay attention to his commands and keep all his decrees, I will not bring on you any of the diseases I brought on the Egyptians, for I am the LORD, who heals you."

EXODUS 15:26

My son, pay attention to what I say;
    turn your ear to my words.
Do not let them out of your sight,
    keep them within your heart;
for they are life to those who find them
    and health to one's whole body.

PROVERBS 4:20–22

Their Loved Ones Don't Understand Them

———◆———

Love must be sincere. Hate what is evil; cling to what is good. Be devoted to one another in love. Honor one another above yourselves.

ROMANS 12:9–10

Like apples of gold in settings of silver
    is a ruling rightly given.
Like an earring of gold or an ornament of fine gold
    is the rebuke of a wise judge to a listening
        ear. . . .
Through patience a ruler can be persuaded,
    and a gentle tongue can break a bone.

PROVERBS 25:11–12, 15

If I speak in the tongues of men or of angels, but do not have love, I am only a resounding gong or a clanging cymbal. If I have the gift of prophecy and can fathom all mysteries and all knowledge, and if I have a faith that can move mountains, but do not have love, I am nothing. If I give all I possess to the poor and give over my body to hardship that I may boast, but do not have love, I gain nothing.

1 Corinthians 13:1–3

Finally, all of you, be like-minded, be sympathetic, love one another, be compassionate and humble. Do not repay evil with evil or insult with insult. On the contrary, repay evil with blessing, because to this you were called so that you may inherit a blessing. For,

"Whoever would love life
    and see good days
must keep their tongue from evil
    and their lips from deceitful speech.
They must turn from evil and do good;
    they must seek peace and pursue it."

1 Peter 3:8–11

Great is our Lord and mighty in power;
 his understanding has no limit.

PSALM 147:5

The LORD will surely comfort Zion
 and will look with compassion on all her ruins;
he will make her deserts like Eden,
 her wastelands like the garden of the LORD.
Joy and gladness will be found in her,
 thanksgiving and the sound of singing. . . .

Lift up your eyes to the heavens,
 look at the earth beneath;
the heavens will vanish like smoke,
 the earth will wear out like a garment
 and its inhabitants die like flies.
But my salvation will last forever,
 my righteousness will never fail.

ISAIAH 51:3, 6

They Must Discipline Their Loved Ones

—◆—

My son, do not despise the LORD's discipline,
    and do not resent his rebuke,
because the LORD disciplines those he loves,
    as a father the son he delights in.

PROVERBS 3:11–12

Moreover, we have all had human fathers who disciplined us and we respected them for it. How much more should we submit to the Father of spirits and live! They disciplined us for a little while as they thought best; but God disciplines us for our good, in order that we may share in his holiness. No discipline seems pleasant at the time, but painful. Later on, however, it produces a harvest of righteousness and peace for those who have been trained by it.

HEBREWS 12:9–11

A rod and a reprimand impart wisdom,
    but a child left undisciplined disgraces its
        mother.

When the wicked thrive, so does sin,
    but the righteous will see their downfall.

Discipline your children, and they will give you
        peace;
    they will bring you the delights you desire.

PROVERBS 29:15–17

Yet now I am happy, not because you were made sorry, but because your sorrow led you to repentance. For you became sorrowful as God intended and so were not harmed in any way by us.

2 CORINTHIANS 7:9

Hatred stirs up conflict,
    but love covers over all wrongs.

Wisdom is found on the lips of the discerning,
    but a rod is for the back of one who has no sense.

PROVERBS 10:12–13

Discipline your children, for in that there is hope;
do not be a willing party to their death.

PROVERBS 19:18

Whoever loves discipline loves knowledge,
but whoever hates correction is stupid.

Good people obtain favor from the LORD,
but he condemns those who devise wicked
schemes.

No one can be established through wickedness,
but the righteous cannot be uprooted.

PROVERBS 12:1–3

My son, keep my words
and store up my commands within you.
Keep my commands and you will live;
guard my teachings as the apple of your eye.
Bind them on your fingers;
write them on the tablet of your heart.

PROVERBS 7:1–3

They Feel Powerless to Protect Their Loved Ones from Evil

———◈———

In the way of righteousness there is life;
    along that path is immortality.

PROVERBS 12:28

Wine is a mocker and beer a brawler;
    whoever is led astray by them is not wise.

PROVERBS 20:1

The violence of the wicked will drag them away,
    for they refuse to do what is right.

PROVERBS 21:7

Through love and faithfulness sin is atoned for;
    through the fear of the LORD evil is avoided.

PROVERBS 16:6

My son, if you accept my words
  and store up my commands within you,
turning your ear to wisdom
  and applying your heart to understanding—
indeed, if you call out for insight
  and cry aloud for understanding,
and if you look for it as for silver
  and search for it as for hidden treasure,
then you will understand the fear of the LORD
  and find the knowledge of God.
For the LORD gives wisdom;
  from his mouth come knowledge and
    understanding.
He holds success in store for the upright,
  he is a shield to those whose walk is blameless,
for he guards the course of the just
  and protects the way of his faithful ones.

Then you will understand what is right and just
  and fair—every good path.

PROVERBS 2:1–9

Don't you know that you yourselves are God's temple and that God's Spirit dwells in your midst? If anyone destroys God's temple, God will destroy that person; for God's temple is sacred, and you together are that temple.

1 CORINTHIANS 3:16–17

"Do not be afraid of those who kill the body but cannot kill the soul. Rather, be afraid of the One who can destroy both soul and body in hell. Are not two sparrows sold for a penny? Yet not one of them will fall to the ground outside your Father's care. And even the very hairs of your head are all numbered. So don't be afraid; you are worth more than many sparrows."

MATTHEW 10:28–31

God's Love Is *with* Men When . . .

They Bring Their Problems to God

———◆———

"Praise be to you, LORD,
    the God of our father Israel,
    from everlasting to everlasting.
Yours, LORD, is the greatness and the power
    and the glory and the majesty and the splendor,
    for everything in heaven and earth is yours.
Yours, LORD, is the kingdom;
    you are exalted as head over all.
Wealth and honor come from you;
    you are the ruler of all things.
In your hands are strength and power
    to exalt and give strength to all.
Now, our God, we give you thanks,
    and praise your glorious name.

1 CHRONICLES 29:10–13

Ah, Sovereign LORD, you have made the heavens and the earth by your great power and outstretched arm. Nothing is too hard for you.

JEREMIAH 32:17

[God will] give relief to you who are troubled, and to us as well. This will happen when the Lord Jesus is revealed from heaven in blazing fire with his powerful angels. He will punish those who do not know God and do not obey the gospel of our Lord Jesus. They will be punished with everlasting destruction and shut out from the presence of the Lord and from the glory of his might on the day he comes to be glorified in his holy people and to be marveled at among all those who have believed. This includes you, because you believed our testimony to you.

With this in mind, we constantly pray for you, that our God may make you worthy of his calling, and that by his power he may bring to fruition your every desire for goodness and your every deed prompted by faith. We pray this so that the name of our Lord Jesus may be glorified in you, and you in him, according to the grace of our God and the Lord Jesus Christ.

2 THESSALONIANS 1:7–12

The Spirit of the Sovereign LORD is on me,
  because the LORD has anointed me
  to proclaim good news to the poor.
He has sent me to bind up the brokenhearted,
  to proclaim freedom for the captives
  and release from darkness for the prisoners,
to proclaim the year of the LORD's favor
  and the day of vengeance of our God,
to comfort all who mourn,
  and provide for those who grieve in Zion—
to bestow on them a crown of beauty
  instead of ashes,
the oil of joy
  instead of mourning,
and a garment of praise
  instead of a spirit of despair.
They will be called oaks of righteousness,
  a planting of the LORD
  for the display of his splendor.

ISAIAH 61:1–3

"For the eyes of the Lord are on the righteous
　　and his ears are attentive to their prayer,
but the face of the Lord is against those who
　　do evil."

Who is going to harm you if you are eager to do good? But even if you should suffer for what is right, you are blessed. "Do not fear their threats; do not be frightened." But in your hearts revere Christ as Lord. Always be prepared to give an answer to everyone who asks you to give the reason for the hope that you have. But do this with gentleness and respect.

1 PETER 3:12–15

It is God who arms me with strength
　　and keeps my way secure.
He makes my feet like the feet of a deer;
　　he causes me to stand on the heights.
He trains my hands for battle;
　　my arms can bend a bow of bronze.
You make your saving help my shield;
　　your help has made me great.
You provide a broad path for my feet,
　　so that my ankles do not give way.

2 SAMUEL 22:33–37

We are hard pressed on every side, but not crushed; perplexed, but not in despair; persecuted, but not abandoned; struck down, but not destroyed. We always carry around in our body the death of Jesus, so that the life of Jesus may also be revealed in our body. . . .

All this is for your benefit, so that the grace that is reaching more and more people may cause thanksgiving to overflow to the glory of God.

Therefore we do not lose heart. Though outwardly we are wasting away, yet inwardly we are being renewed day by day. For our light and momentary troubles are achieving for us an eternal glory that far outweighs them all. So we fix our eyes not on what is seen, but on what is unseen, since what is seen is temporary, but what is unseen is eternal.

2 Corinthians 4:8–10, 15–18

Reflect on what I am saying, for the Lord will give you insight into all this. . . .

Here is a trustworthy saying:
If we died with him,
    we will also live with him;
if we endure,
    we will also reign with him.
If we disown him,
    he will also disown us;
if we are faithless,
    he remains faithful,
    for he cannot disown himself.

2 TIMOTHY 2:7, 11–13

They Rely on God to Guide Their Lives

My son, keep your father's command
    and do not forsake your mother's teaching.
Bind them always on your heart;
    fasten them around your neck.
When you walk, they will guide you;
    when you sleep, they will watch over you;
    when you awake, they will speak to you.
For this command is a lamp,
    this teaching is a light,
and correction and instruction
    are the way to life.

PROVERBS 6:20–23

My dear children, I write this to you so that you will not sin. But if anybody does sin, we have an advocate with the Father—Jesus Christ, the Righteous One. He is the atoning sacrifice for our sins, and not only for ours but also for the sins of the whole world.

1 JOHN 2:1–2

Do you not know?
    Have you not heard?
The LORD is the everlasting God,
    the Creator of the ends of the earth.
He will not grow tired or weary,
    and his understanding no one can fathom.
He gives strength to the weary
    and increases the power of the weak.
Even youths grow tired and weary,
    and young men stumble and fall;
but those who hope in the LORD
    will renew their strength.
They will soar on wings like eagles;
    they will run and not grow weary,
    they will walk and not be faint.

ISAIAH 40:28–31

"I will go before you
    and will level the mountains;
I will break down gates of bronze
    and cut through bars of iron.
I will give you hidden treasures,
    riches stored in secret places,
so that you may know that I am the LORD,
    the God of Israel, who summons you by name."

ISAIAH 45:2–3

"Forget the former things;
    do not dwell on the past.
See, I am doing a new thing!
    Now it springs up; do you not perceive it?
I am making a way in the wilderness
    and streams in the wasteland."

ISAIAH 43:18–19

"So do not fear, for I am with you;
    do not be dismayed, for I am your God.
I will strengthen you and help you;
    I will uphold you with my righteous right hand."

ISAIAH 41:10

"As the rain and the snow
      come down from heaven,
and do not return to it
      without watering the earth
and making it bud and flourish,
      so that it yields seed for the sower and bread for
            the eater,
so is my word that goes out from my mouth:
      It will not return to me empty,
but will accomplish what I desire
      and achieve the purpose for which I sent it."

                                        ISAIAH 55:10–11

"Though the mountains be shaken
      and the hills be removed,
yet my unfailing love for you will not be shaken
      nor my covenant of peace be removed,"
      says the LORD, who has compassion on you.

                                        ISAIAH 54:10

They Share Their Good Fortune with Others

——◆——

Give generously to them and do so without a grudging heart; then because of this the LORD your God will bless you in all your work and in everything you put your hand to. There will always be poor people in the land. Therefore I command you to be openhanded toward your fellow Israelites who are poor and needy in your land.

DEUTERONOMY 15:10–11

"Give, and it will be given to you. A good measure, pressed down, shaken together and running over, will be poured into your lap. For with the measure you use, it will be measured to you."

LUKE 6:38

The LORD sends poverty and wealth;
    he humbles and he exalts.
He raises the poor from the dust
    and lifts the needy from the ash heap;
he seats them with princes
    and has them inherit a throne of honor.

For the foundations of the earth are the LORD's;
    on them he has set the world.

1 SAMUEL 2:7–8

Whoever oppresses the poor shows contempt for
        their Maker,
    but whoever is kind to the needy honors God.

PROVERBS 14:31

What good is it, my brothers . . . if someone claims to have faith but has no deeds? Can such faith save them? Suppose a brother or a sister is without clothes and daily food. If one of you says to them, "Go in peace; keep warm and well fed," but does nothing about their physical needs, what good is it? In the same way, faith by itself, if it is not accompanied by action, is dead.

JAMES 2:14–17

Jesus answered, "If you want to be perfect, go, sell your possessions and give to the poor, and you will have treasure in heaven. Then come, follow me."

When the young man heard this, he went away sad, because he had great wealth.

Then Jesus said to his disciples, "Truly I tell you, it is hard for someone who is rich to enter the kingdom of heaven. Again I tell you, it is easier for a camel to go through the eye of a needle than for someone who is rich to enter the kingdom of God."

MATTHEW 19:21–24

They Pray with Their Families

———◆———

The LORD is near to all who call on him,
to all who call on him in truth.
He fulfills the desires of those who fear him;
he hears their cry and saves them.

PSALM 145:18–19

Rejoice in the Lord always. I will say it again: Rejoice! Let your gentleness be evident to all. The Lord is near. Do not be anxious about anything, but in every situation, by prayer and petition, with thanksgiving, present your requests to God. And the peace of God, which transcends all understanding, will guard your hearts and your minds in Christ Jesus.

PHILIPPIANS 4:4–7

"Call to me and I will answer you and tell you great and unsearchable things you do not know."

Jeremiah 33:3

Many will give thanks on our behalf for the gracious favor granted us in answer to the prayers of many.

Now this is our boast: Our conscience testifies that we have conducted ourselves in the world, and especially in our relations with you, with integrity and godly sincerity. We have done so, relying not on worldly wisdom but on God's grace. For we do not write you anything you cannot read or understand. And I hope that, as you have understood us in part, you will come to understand fully that you can boast of us just as we will boast of you in the day of the Lord Jesus.

2 Corinthians 1:11–14

"Again, truly I tell you that if two of you on earth agree about anything they ask for, it will be done for them by my Father in heaven. For where two or three gather in my name, there am I with them."

Matthew 18:19–20

"If you believe, you will receive whatever you ask for in prayer."

Let us then approach God's throne of grace with confidence, so that we may receive mercy and find grace to help us in our time of need.

HEBREWS 4:16

Now, our God, hear the prayers and petitions of your servant. For your sake, Lord, look with favor on your desolate sanctuary. Give ear, our God, and hear; open your eyes and see the desolation of the city that bears your Name. We do not make requests of you because we are righteous, but because of your great mercy. Lord, listen! Lord, forgive! Lord, hear and act! For your sake, my God, do not delay, because your city and your people bear your Name.

DANIEL 9:17–19

They Forgive Those Who Have Offended Them

Then Peter came to Jesus and asked, "Lord, how many times shall I forgive my brother or sister who sins against me? Up to seven times?"

Jesus answered, "I tell you, not seven times, but seventy-seven times."

MATTHEW 18:21–22

"So watch yourselves.

"If your brother or sister sins against you, rebuke them; and if they repent, forgive them. Even if they sin against you seven times in a day and seven times come back to you saying 'I repent,' you must forgive them."

LUKE 17:3–4

He made known his ways to Moses,
>his deeds to the people of Israel:

The LORD is compassionate and gracious,
>slow to anger, abounding in love.

He will not always accuse,
>nor will he harbor his anger forever;

he does not treat us as our sins deserve
>or repay us according to our iniquities.

For as high as the heavens are above the earth,
>so great is his love for those who fear him;

as far as the east is from the west,
>so far has he removed our transgressions from us.

As a father has compassion on his children,
>so the LORD has compassion on those who
>>fear him.

PSALM 103:7–13

"For if you forgive other people when they sin against you, your heavenly Father will also forgive you. But if you do not forgive others their sins, your Father will not forgive your sins."

MATTHEW 6:14–15

"But love your enemies, do good to them, and lend to them without expecting to get anything back. Then your reward will be great, and you will be children of the Most High, because he is kind to the ungrateful and wicked. Be merciful, just as your Father is merciful.

"Do not judge, and you will not be judged. Do not condemn, and you will not be condemned. Forgive, and you will be forgiven."

LUKE 6:35–37

"And when you stand praying, if you hold anything against anyone, forgive them, so that your Father in heaven may forgive you your sins."

MARK 11:25

God Rejoices

When Men . . .

Anticipate Christ's Return

See what great love the Father has lavished on us, that we should be called children of God! And that is what we are! The reason the world does not know us is that it did not know him. Dear friends, now we are children of God, and what we will be has not yet been made known. But we know that when Christ appears, we shall be like him, for we shall see him as he is. All who have this hope in him purify themselves, just as he is pure.

1 JOHN 3:1–3

"Do not let your hearts be troubled. You believe in God; believe also in me. My Father's house has many rooms; if that were not so, would I have told you that I am going there to prepare a place for you? And if I go and prepare a place for you, I will come back and take you to be with me that you also may be where I am."

JOHN 14:1–3

Those the LORD has rescued will return.
  They will enter Zion with singing;
  everlasting joy will crown their heads.
Gladness and joy will overtake them,
  and sorrow and sighing will flee away.

ISAIAH 51:11

"See, I will create
  new heavens and a new earth.
The former things will not be remembered,
  nor will they come to mind.
But be glad and rejoice forever
  in what I will create,
for I will create Jerusalem to be a delight
  and its people a joy.
I will rejoice over Jerusalem
  and take delight in my people;
the sound of weeping and of crying
  will be heard in it no more."

ISAIAH 65:17–19

"For as lightning that comes from the east is visible even in the west, so will be the coming of the Son of Man. Wherever there is a carcass, there the vultures will gather.

"Immediately after the distress of those days

"'the sun will be darkened,
    and the moon will not give its light;
the stars will fall from the sky,
    and the heavenly bodies will be shaken.'

"Then will appear the sign of the Son of Man in heaven. And then all the peoples of the earth will mourn when they see the Son of Man coming on the clouds of heaven, with power and great glory. And he will send his angels with a loud trumpet call, and they will gather his elect from the four winds, from one end of the heavens to the other."

Matthew 24:27–31

While we wait for the blessed hope—the appearing of the glory of our great God and Savior, Jesus Christ, who gave himself for us to redeem us from all wickedness and to purify for himself a people that are his very own, eager to do what is good.

Titus 2:13–14

"There will be signs in the sun, moon and stars. On the earth, nations will be in anguish and perplexity at the roaring and tossing of the sea. People will faint from terror, apprehensive of what is coming on the world, for the heavenly bodies will be shaken. At that time they will see the Son of Man coming in a cloud with power and great glory. When these things begin to take place, stand up and lift up your heads, because your redemption is drawing near."

LUKE 21:25–28

But the day of the Lord will come like a thief. The heavens will disappear with a roar; the elements will be destroyed by fire, and the earth and everything done in it will be laid bare.

Since everything will be destroyed in this way, what kind of people ought you to be? You ought to live holy and godly lives as you look forward to the day of God and speed its coming. That day will bring about the destruction of the heavens by fire, and the elements will melt in the heat.

2 PETER 3:10–12

Whoever believes in the Son of God accepts this testimony. Whoever does not believe God has made him out to be a liar, because they have not believed the testimony God has given about his Son. And this is the testimony: God has given us eternal life, and this life is in his Son. Whoever has the Son has life; whoever does not have the Son of God does not have life.

I write these things to you who believe in the name of the Son of God so that you may know that you have eternal life.

1 John 5:10–13

"'He will wipe every tear from their eyes. There will be no more death' or mourning or crying or pain, for the old order of things has passed away."

Revelation 21:4

Dedicate Their Lives to God

So in Christ Jesus you are all children of God through faith, for all of you who were baptized into Christ have clothed yourselves with Christ. There is neither Jew nor Gentile, neither slave nor free, nor is there male and female, for you are all one in Christ Jesus. If you belong to Christ, then you are Abraham's seed, and heirs according to the promise.

GALATIANS 3:26–29

"Very truly I tell you, whoever believes in me will do the works I have been doing, and they will do even greater things than these, because I am going to the Father. And I will do whatever you ask in my name, so that the Father may be glorified in the Son. You may ask me for anything in my name, and I will do it."

JOHN 14:12–14

"I am the vine; you are the branches. If you remain in me and I in you, you will bear much fruit; apart from me you can do nothing. If you do not remain in me, you are like a branch that is thrown away and withers; such branches are picked up, thrown into the fire and burned. If you remain in me and my words remain in you, ask whatever you wish, and it will be done for you. This is to my Father's glory, that you bear much fruit, showing yourselves to be my disciples."

JOHN 15:5–8

"You did not choose me, but I chose you and appointed you so that you might go and bear fruit—fruit that will last—and so that whatever you ask in my name the Father will give you. This is my command: Love each other."

JOHN 15:16–17

"In that day you will no longer ask me anything. Very truly I tell you, my Father will give you whatever you ask in my name. Until now you have not asked for anything in my name. Ask and you will receive, and your joy will be complete."

JOHN 16:23–24

Walk in the way of love, just as Christ loved us and gave himself up for us as a fragrant offering and sacrifice to God. . . .

For you were once darkness, but now you are light in the Lord. Live as children of light (for the fruit of the light consists in all goodness, righteousness and truth) and find out what pleases the Lord.

EPHESIANS 5:2, 8–10

Therefore we are always confident and know that as long as we are at home in the body we are away from the Lord. For we live by faith, not by sight. We are confident, I say, and would prefer to be away from the body and at home with the Lord. So we make it our goal to please him, whether we are at home in the body or away from it. For we must all appear before the judgment seat of Christ, so that each of us may receive what is due us for the things done while in the body, whether good or bad.

2 CORINTHIANS 5:6–10

Trust and Wait for God's Answers

—◆—

"Because the poor are plundered and the needy
      groan,
   I will now arise," says the LORD.
   "I will protect them from those who malign
      them."
And the words of the LORD are flawless,
   like silver purified in a crucible,
   like gold refined seven times.

You, LORD, will keep the needy safe
   and will protect us forever from the wicked,
who freely strut about
   when what is vile is honored by the human race.

PSALM 12:5–8

Every word of God is flawless;
he is a shield to those who take refuge in him.

PROVERBS 30:5

Don't be deceived, my dear brothers. . . . Every good
and perfect gift is from above, coming down from the
Father of the heavenly lights, who does not change
like shifting shadows.

JAMES 1:16–17

Commit your way to the LORD;
trust in him and he will do this:
He will make your righteous reward shine like
the dawn,
your vindication like the noonday sun.

Be still before the LORD
and wait patiently for him.

PSALM 37:5–7

I will wait for the LORD,
who is hiding his face from the descendants
of Jacob.
I will put my trust in him.

ISAIAH 8:17

"I am the LORD, and there is no other;
    apart from me there is no God.
I will strengthen you,
    though you have not acknowledged me,
so that from the rising of the sun
    to the place of its setting
people may know there is none besides me.
    I am the LORD, and there is no other."

ISAIAH 45:5–6

Comfort, comfort my people,
    says your God.
Speak tenderly to Jerusalem,
    and proclaim to her
that her hard service has been completed,
    that her sin has been paid for,
that she has received from the LORD's hand
    double for all her sins.

A voice of one calling:
"In the wilderness prepare
    the way for the LORD;
make straight in the desert
    a highway for our God."

ISAIAH 40:1–3

You will keep in perfect peace
   those whose minds are steadfast,
   because they trust in you.
Trust in the LORD forever,
   for the LORD, the LORD himself, is the Rock
      eternal.

ISAIAH 26:3–4

The LORD your God is with you,
   the Mighty Warrior who saves.
He will take great delight in you;
   in his love he will no longer rebuke you,
   but will rejoice over you with singing.

ZEPHANIAH 3:17

Are Reconciled with Their Brother

——◇——

For he himself is our peace, who has made the two groups one and has destroyed the barrier, the dividing wall of hostility, by setting aside in his flesh the law with its commands and regulations. His purpose was to create in himself one new humanity out of the two, thus making peace, and in one body to reconcile both of them to God through the cross, by which he put to death their hostility. He came and preached peace to you who were far away and peace to those who were near. For through him we both have access to the Father by one Spirit.

EPHESIANS 2:14–18

"If your brother or sister sins, go and point out their fault, just between the two of you. If they listen to you, you have won them over."

MATTHEW 18:15

Jesus replied: "'Love the Lord your God with all your heart and with all your soul and with all your mind.' This is the first and greatest commandment. And the second is like it: 'Love your neighbor as yourself.' All the Law and the Prophets hang on these two commandments."

MATTHEW 22:37–40

"I have given them the glory that you gave me, that they may be one as we are one—I in them and you in me—so that they may be brought to complete unity. Then the world will know that you sent me and have loved them even as you have loved me."

JOHN 17:22–23

We are therefore Christ's ambassadors, as though God were making his appeal through us. We implore you on Christ's behalf: Be reconciled to God. God made him who had no sin to be sin for us, so that in him we might become the righteousness of God.

2 CORINTHIANS 5:20–21

How good and pleasant it is
    when God's people live together in unity!

It is like precious oil poured on the head,
    running down on the beard,
running down on Aaron's beard,
    down on the collar of his robe.
It is as if the dew of Hermon
    were falling on Mount Zion.
For there the Lord bestows his blessing,
    even life forevermore.

Psalm 133:1–3

For if, while we were God's enemies, we were reconciled to him through the death of his Son, how much more, having been reconciled, shall we be saved through his life! Not only is this so, but we also boast in God through our Lord Jesus Christ, through whom we have now received reconciliation.

Romans 5:10–11

Dynamic
Examples *of*
Godly Men

Abraham

---◆---

The LORD had said to Abram, "Go from your country, your people and your father's household to the land I will show you.

"I will make you into a great nation,
and I will bless you;
I will make your name great,
and you will be a blessing.
I will bless those who bless you,
and whoever curses you I will curse;
and all peoples on earth
will be blessed through you."

GENESIS 12:1–3

After this, the word of the LORD came to Abram in a vision:

"Do not be afraid, Abram.
I am your shield,
your very great reward."

But Abram said, "Sovereign LORD, what can you give me since I remain childless and the one who will inherit my estate is Eliezer of Damascus?" And Abram said, "You have given me no children; so a servant in my household will be my heir."

Then the word of the LORD came to him: "This man will not be your heir, but a son who is your own flesh and blood will be your heir." He took him outside and said, "Look up at the sky and count the stars—if indeed you can count them." Then he said to him, "So shall your offspring be."

Abram believed the LORD, and he credited it to him as righteousness.

GENESIS 15:1–6

The Lord said to Abram after Lot had parted from him, "Look around from where you are, to the north and south, to the east and west. All the land that you see I will give to you and your offspring forever. I will make your offspring like the dust of the earth, so that if anyone could count the dust, then your offspring could be counted."

GENESIS 13:14–16

Understand, then, that those who have faith are children of Abraham. Scripture foresaw that God would justify the Gentiles by faith, and announced the gospel in advance to Abraham: "All nations will be blessed through you." So those who rely on faith are blessed along with Abraham, the man of faith.

GALATIANS 3:7–9

Jacob

Sing for joy to God our strength;
 shout aloud to the God of Jacob!
Begin the music, strike the timbrel,
 play the melodious harp and lyre.

Sound the ram's horn at the New Moon,
 and when the moon is full, on the day of our
  festival;
this is a decree for Israel,
 an ordinance of the God of Jacob. . . .

I am the LORD your God,
 who brought you up out of Egypt.
Open wide your mouth and I will fill it.

PSALM 81:1–4, 10

Then God said to Jacob, "Go up to Bethel and settle there, and build an altar there to God, who appeared to you when you were fleeing from your brother Esau."

So Jacob said to his household and to all who were with him, "Get rid of the foreign gods you have with you, and purify yourselves and change your clothes. Then come, let us go up to Bethel, where I will build an altar to God, who answered me in the day of my distress and who has been with me wherever I have gone."

GENESIS 35:1–3

They took the ornate robe back to their father and said, "We found this. Examine it to see whether it is your son's robe."

He recognized it and said, "It is my son's robe! Some ferocious animal has devoured him. Joseph has surely been torn to pieces."

Then Jacob tore his clothes, put on sackcloth and mourned for his son many days. All his sons and daughters came to comfort him, but he refused to be comforted. "No," he said, "I will continue to mourn until I join my son in the grave." So his father wept for him.

GENESIS 37:32–35

So Jacob was left alone, and a man wrestled with him till daybreak. When the man saw that he could not overpower him, he touched the socket of Jacob's hip so that his hip was wrenched as he wrestled with the man. Then the man said, "Let me go, for it is daybreak."

But Jacob replied, "I will not let you go unless you bless me."

The man asked him, "What is your name?"

"Jacob," he answered.

Then the man said, "Your name will no longer be Jacob, but Israel, because you have struggled with God and with humans and have overcome."

Jacob said, "Please tell me your name."

But he replied, "Why do you ask my name?" Then he blessed him there.

So Jacob called the place Peniel, saying, "It is because I saw God face to face, and yet my life was spared."

GENESIS 32:24–30

Joseph

—◆—

Joseph threw himself on his father and wept over him and kissed him.

GENESIS 50:1

When Israel saw the sons of Joseph, he asked, "Who are these?"

"They are the sons God has given me here," Joseph said to his father.

Then Israel said, "Bring them to me so I may bless them."

Now Israel's eyes were failing because of old age, and he could hardly see. So Joseph brought his sons close to him, and his father kissed them and embraced them.

GENESIS 48:8–10

Before the years of famine came, two sons were born to Joseph by Asenath daughter of Potiphera, priest of On. Joseph named his firstborn Manasseh and said, "It is because God has made me forget all my trouble and all my father's household." The second son he named Ephraim and said, "It is because God has made me fruitful in the land of my suffering."

The seven years of abundance in Egypt came to an end, and the seven years of famine began, just as Joseph had said. There was famine in all the other lands, but in the whole land of Egypt there was food. When all Egypt began to feel the famine, the people cried to Pharaoh for food. Then Pharaoh told all the Egyptians, "Go to Joseph and do what he tells you."

When the famine had spread over the whole country, Joseph opened all the storehouses and sold grain to the Egyptians, for the famine was severe throughout Egypt. And all the world came to Egypt to buy grain from Joseph, because the famine was severe everywhere.

Genesis 41:50–57

Then Joseph could no longer control himself before all his attendants, and he cried out, "Have everyone leave my presence!" So there was no one with Joseph when he made himself known to his brothers. And he wept so loudly that the Egyptians heard him, and Pharaoh's household heard about it.

Joseph said to his brothers, "I am Joseph! Is my father still living?" But his brothers were not able to answer him, because they were terrified at his presence.

Then Joseph said to his brothers, "Come close to me." When they had done so, he said, "I am your brother Joseph, the one you sold into Egypt! And now, do not be distressed and do not be angry with yourselves for selling me here, because it was to save lives that God sent me ahead of you. For two years now there has been famine in the land, and for the next five years there will be no plowing and reaping. But God sent me ahead of you to preserve for you a remnant on earth and to save your lives by a great deliverance.

"So then, it was not you who sent me here, but God. He made me father to Pharaoh, lord of his entire household and ruler of all Egypt. Now hurry back to my father and say to him, 'This is what your son Joseph says: God has made me lord of all Egypt. Come down to me; don't delay. You shall live in the region of Goshen and be near me—you, your children and grandchildren, your flocks and herds, and all you have.'"

GENESIS 45:1–10

Joseph also provided his father and his brothers and all his father's household with food, according to the number of their children.

GENESIS 47:12

David

—◆—

"As for you, if you walk before me faithfully as David your father did, and do all I command, and observe my decrees and laws, I will establish your royal throne, as I covenanted with David your father when I said, 'You shall never fail to have a successor to rule over Israel.'"

2 CHRONICLES 7:17–18

Give ear and come to me;
    listen, that you may live.
I will make an everlasting covenant with you,
    my faithful love promised to David.
See, I have made him a witness to the peoples,
    a ruler and commander of the peoples.

ISAIAH 55:3–4

David sang to the LORD the words of this song when the LORD delivered him from the hand of all his enemies and from the hand of Saul. . . .

"You, LORD, are my lamp;
　　the LORD turns my darkness into light.
With your help I can advance against a troop;
　　with my God I can scale a wall.

"As for God, his way is perfect:
　　The LORD's word is flawless;
　　he shields all who take refuge in him.
For who is God besides the LORD?
　　And who is the Rock except our God?
It is God who arms me with strength
　　and keeps my way secure.
He makes my feet like the feet of a deer;
　　he causes me to stand on the heights.
He trains my hands for battle;
　　my arms can bend a bow of bronze.
You make your saving help my shield;
　　your help has made me great."

2 SAMUEL 22:1, 29–36

For the sake of your servant David,
    do not reject your anointed one.

The LORD swore an oath to David,
    a sure oath he will not revoke:
"One of your own descendants
    I will place on your throne.
If your sons keep my covenant
    and the statutes I teach them,
then their sons will sit
    on your throne for ever and ever."

For the LORD has chosen Zion,
    he has desired it for his dwelling, saying,
"This is my resting place for ever and ever;
    here I will sit enthroned, for I have desired it.
I will bless her with abundant provisions;
    her poor I will satisfy with food.
I will clothe her priests with salvation,
    and her faithful people will ever sing for joy.

"Here I will make a horn grow for David
    and set up a lamp for my anointed one.
I will clothe his enemies with shame,
    but his head will be adorned with a radiant crown."

PSALM 132:10–18

Achish replied, "Is this not David, who was an officer of Saul king of Israel? He has already been with me for over a year, and from the day he left Saul until now, I have found no fault in him." . . .

So Achish called David and said to him, "As surely as the Lord lives, you have been reliable. . . . From the day you came to me until today, I have found no fault in you."

1 Samuel 29:3, 6

Noah

———◆———

The LORD then said to Noah, "Go into the ark, you and your whole family, because I have found you righteous in this generation. . . ."

Noah was six hundred years old when the floodwaters came on the earth. And Noah and his sons and his wife and his sons' wives entered the ark to escape the waters of the flood. Pairs of clean and unclean animals, of birds and of all creatures that move along the ground, male and female, came to Noah and entered the ark, as God had commanded Noah. And after the seven days the floodwaters came on the earth.

GENESIS 7:1, 6–10

But God remembered Noah and all the wild animals and the livestock that were with him in the ark, and he sent a wind over the earth, and the waters receded.

GENESIS 8:1

So the LORD said, "I will wipe from the face of the earth the human race I have created—and with them the animals, the birds and the creatures that move along the ground—for I regret that I have made them." But Noah found favor in the eyes of the LORD.

This is the account of Noah and his family.

Noah was a righteous man, blameless among the people of his time, and he walked faithfully with God. Noah had three sons: Shem, Ham and Japheth.

GENESIS 6:7–10

And without faith it is impossible to please God, because anyone who comes to him must believe that he exists and that he rewards those who earnestly seek him.

By faith Noah, when warned about things not yet seen, in holy fear built an ark to save his family. By his faith he condemned the world and became heir of the righteousness that is in keeping with faith.

HEBREWS 11:6–7

Paul

As he neared Damascus on his journey, suddenly a light from heaven flashed around him. He fell to the ground and heard a voice say to him, "Saul, Saul, why do you persecute me?"

"Who are you, Lord?" Saul asked.

"I am Jesus, whom you are persecuting," he replied. "Now get up and go into the city, and you will be told what you must do."

The men traveling with Saul stood there speechless; they heard the sound but did not see anyone. Saul got up from the ground, but when he opened his eyes he could see nothing. So they led him by the hand into Damascus. For three days he was blind, and did not eat or drink anything.

ACTS 9:3–9

About midnight Paul and Silas were praying and singing hymns to God, and the other prisoners were listening to them. Suddenly there was such a violent earthquake that the foundations of the prison were shaken. At once all the prison doors flew open, and everyone's chains came loose. The jailer woke up, and when he saw the prison doors open, he drew his sword and was about to kill himself because he thought the prisoners had escaped. But Paul shouted, "Don't harm yourself! We are all here!"

The jailer called for lights, rushed in and fell trembling before Paul and Silas. He then brought them out and asked, "Sirs, what must I do to be saved?"

They replied, "Believe in the Lord Jesus, and you will be saved—you and your household." Then they spoke the word of the Lord to him and to all the others in his house. At that hour of the night the jailer took them and washed their wounds; then immediately he and all his household were baptized. The jailer brought them into his house and set a meal before them; he was filled with joy because he had come to believe in God—he and his whole household.

ACTS 16:25–34

I consider that our present sufferings are not worth comparing with the glory that will be revealed in us. For the creation waits in eager expectation for the children of God to be revealed. For the creation was subjected to frustration, not by its own choice, but by the will of the one who subjected it, in hope that the creation itself will be liberated from its bondage to decay and brought into the freedom and glory of the children of God.

We know that the whole creation has been groaning as in the pains of childbirth right up to the present time. Not only so, but we ourselves, who have the firstfruits of the Spirit, groan inwardly as we wait eagerly for our adoption to sonship, the redemption of our bodies. For in this hope we were saved. But hope that is seen is no hope at all. Who hopes for what they already have? But if we hope for what we do not yet have, we wait for it patiently.

In the same way, the Spirit helps us in our weakness. We do not know what we ought to pray for, but the Spirit himself intercedes for us through wordless groans. And he who searches our hearts knows the mind of the Spirit, because the Spirit intercedes for God's people in accordance with the will of God.

ROMANS 8:18–27

Are they Hebrews? So am I. Are they Israelites? So am I. Are they Abraham's descendants? So am I. Are they servants of Christ? (I am out of my mind to talk like this.) I am more. I have worked much harder, been in prison more frequently, been flogged more severely, and been exposed to death again and again. Five times I received from the Jews the forty lashes minus one. Three times I was beaten with rods, once I was pelted with stones, three times I was shipwrecked, I spent a night and a day in the open sea, I have been constantly on the move. I have been in danger from rivers, in danger from bandits, in danger from my fellow Jews, in danger from Gentiles; in danger in the city, in danger in the country, in danger at sea; and in danger from false believers. I have labored and toiled and have often gone without sleep; I have known hunger and thirst and have often gone without food; I have been cold and naked. Besides everything else, I face daily the pressure of my concern for all the churches. Who is weak, and I do not feel weak? Who is led into sin, and I do not inwardly burn?

If I must boast, I will boast of the things that show my weakness. The God and Father of the Lord Jesus, who is to be praised forever, knows that I am not lying.

2 Corinthians 11:22–31